THE GREAT IRISH HISTORY BOOK

MYLES DUNGAN

ILLUSTRATED BY ALAN DUNNE

GILL BOOKS

THE AUTHOR

ABOUT MYLES

MYLES DUNGAN is a broadcaster and historian who has written more than a dozen books on Irish and American history and presents *The History Show* every week on RTÉ Radio 1 – that's a radio station your parents might listen to. He has also presented many RTÉ sports programmes wearing very dodgy sweaters, but is trying to forget about that. This is his first book for younger readers and he is very nervous about it.

MYLES'S ACKNOWLEDGEMENTS

Myles would very much like to thank Sarah Liddy and Aoibheann Molumby of Gill Books for asking him to write this book and then showing him how to do it properly. Myles's thanks are also due to his ten-year-old editor, his daughter, Gwyneth Williams, and his fabulous agent, Jonathan Williams (no relation of Gwyneth's).

THE ILLUSTRATOR

ABOUT ALAN

ALAN DUNNE is an illustrator who loves making comics and picture books. He has created illustrations for museums, postage stamps and heritage projects. In a previous life he was a designer for RTÉ Television. He loves reading about history and collecting old illustrated books and newspapers, so illustrating this book was a real joy!

ALAN'S ACKNOWLEDGEMENTS

A huge thank you to Sarah, Aoibheann and all the team at Gill. To Myles Dungan for his funny and enlightening observations on Irish history; it was great fun to illustrate! To Graham Thew for his beautiful design work. To my wife, Gráinne Begley, for all her support, and to our son Tadhg, who can't wait to be a knight when he grows up!

CONTENTS

INTRODUCTION

Ireland has been an independent state for a century now, and although things are far from perfect in 2022, we've made huge strides since we won our independence from Britain a hundred years ago. We've even beaten them at soccer once or twice.

The author himself has officially been an adult (though not a proper 'grown-up') for exactly half of the period of Irish independence. This is probably why he was asked to write this book. His loving family certainly can't think of any other reason.

Since 1922, we have seen a bitter civil war and decades of poverty and emigration, and we (thankfully) managed to sit out World War II on the sidelines. We have also witnessed a vicious 30-year conflict in Northern Ireland and experienced sudden prosperity during the Celtic Tiger.

That was when normally sensible Irish people were buying Jacuzzis and holiday homes in countries whose names they couldn't pronounce.

And that's only the last century!

Prior to that, we were a (sort of) British colony after the Normans arrived in the 12th century. However, we were such a major nuisance that the British were quite happy to be rid of (most of) us in 1922. Before the Norman invasion (our 'Normans' were mostly Welsh, by the way), the country was divided into dozens of tiny warring kingdoms, each dominated by a particular 'clan' who were always trying to put one over on their neighbours. Even after the Normans arrived and offered us a common enemy, we never really lost our talent for taking lumps out of each other. By the 19th century that job

had largely been taken over by the GAA, and (with the exception of the Dublin–Meath rivalry) the number of mass slaughters and beheadings has been greatly reduced, thanks to the All-Ireland football and hurling championships.

Over the next 90 pages or so you'll be expected to cheer on some genuine Irish heroes, like our only Megalosaurus; our patron saint, Patrick; the great northern general Hugh O'Neill; the 'Liberator' Daniel O'Connell; the resourceful Anna Parnell; the courageous nurse, Elizabeth O'Farrell; and the ruthless Michael Collins. You will also probably want to boo and hiss the likes of Dermot MacMurrough, Oliver Cromwell, Leonard McNally and Pierce Nagle. But that's entirely up to you. You may not be nearly as judgemental as the author. You might

be the kind of reader who can see the angel in everyone. Good for you.

In case it isn't obvious, the story of Ireland is not just about a 750-year struggle for political independence. All that revolutionary stuff doesn't really get going properly until 1798. And, of course, many Irish people didn't want independence. They were called (they still are) unionists or loyalists. They prefer to be Irish and British at the same time.

Far more important for decades of Irish history were the many fights about who really owned Irish land. In the 17th century, its original owners, mostly Irish Catholics, had lost their land after a series of terrible wars. It was given to Protestant settlers instead (mostly by Oliver Cromwell – all together now: 'Boo, hiss'). The new owners then became

wealthy landlords, and for over two centuries, Irish farmers paid a lot of rent to people they felt had stolen the land from their ancestors in the first place. They weren't happy until the landlords were all gone. There were many campaigns for rents to be reduced and to prevent landlords from evicting tenants from their farms, but behind all those struggles was the hope that the landlords could be persuaded to sell to their tenants and leave. That didn't finally happen until shortly before Ireland got its independence from Britain. But when it did happen, to many Irish people it was far more important than having our own government.

So keep all that in mind as you go through this volume. And we hope that by reading *The Great Irish History Book* you might be encouraged to read some more books

about our fascinating country. Or go and visit some of our really cool museums. Bring the book with you, why don't you?

Myles Dungan
September 2022

PREHISTORIC IRELAND

Even though it rains a lot in Ireland, count your blessings. Six hundred million years ago we were entirely under water. Not only that – we were in two parts and close to the shores of north-west Africa! All the great (and small) masses of land we live on today are constantly on the move, though you would need to be around for millions of years to actually spot that Ireland is getting further away from Wales all the time. The process by which countries and continents drift apart, and then bang into each other, is called CONTINENTAL DRIFT (not the movie!). It began hundreds of millions of years ago and hasn't stopped.

A MOVING EXPERIENCE

Two hundred million years before the first dinosaurs arrived (about 240,000,00 BC) Ireland started to drift (very, very) slowly northwards. The two parts of our underwater island gradually joined together and emerged from the sea near the EQUATOR – the imaginary line that circles the middle of Earth. By the time the dinosaurs disappeared (about 65 million years ago) – after the earth was hit by a huge asteroid more than 10 kilometres wide – Ireland was getting closer to its current parking place on the western edge of Europe. We finally made it to where we are now (for the moment, at least) about 20 million years ago.

OUR FOSSILISED ANCESTORS

So, because we spent a lot of time underwater during the rule of the dinosaurs, this sadly means that T-Rex may never have roamed freely across the plains of Ireland looking for something tasty to snack on, although fossil evidence of one of his near relatives, a MEGALOSAURUS, has been found in Northern Ireland. Irish fossil remains run more to exotic sea creatures who died out millions of years ago. These include the AMMONOID (a distant relation of the squid) and the CRINOID (ancestor of the starfish), who left plenty of traces of their existence before they followed the dinosaurs into extinction.

240,000,000 BC

65,000,000 BC

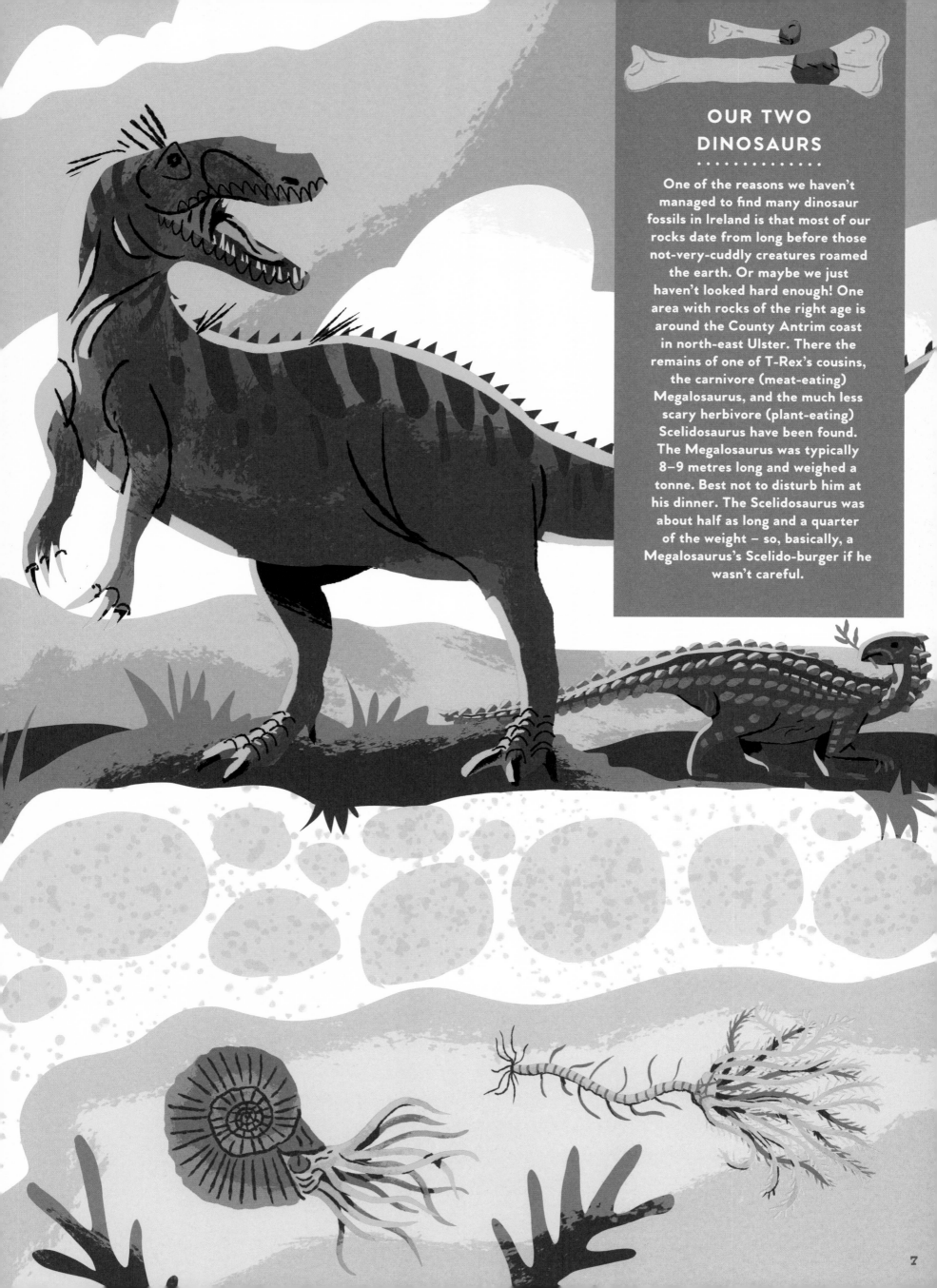

OUR TWO DINOSAURS

One of the reasons we haven't managed to find many dinosaur fossils in Ireland is that most of our rocks date from long before those not-very-cuddly creatures roamed the earth. Or maybe we just haven't looked hard enough! One area with rocks of the right age is around the County Antrim coast in north-east Ulster. There the remains of one of T-Rex's cousins, the carnivore (meat-eating) Megalosaurus, and the much less scary herbivore (plant-eating) Scelidosaurus have been found. The Megalosaurus was typically 8–9 metres long and weighed a tonne. Best not to disturb him at his dinner. The Scelidosaurus was about half as long and a quarter of the weight – so, basically, a Megalosaurus's Scelido-burger if he wasn't careful.

PRE-CHRISTIAN IRELAND

Our most ancient ancestors were hunter-gatherers. They arrived here a few thousand years after the end of the last ICE AGE, when ice covered most of the continent of Europe (so, around 8000 BC) and hunted for their food. They shared the island with some exotic animals that have long since become extinct, such as the woolly mammoth (the hairy elephants who star in *Continental Drift*) and the elk (a species of giant deer with impossibly large antlers). They lived on an island almost completely covered by trees, which they would have chopped down with tools mostly made of flint, a rock that can easily be cut into sharp points and edges.

ASHES TO ASHES

Gradually the hunter-gatherers began to settle down and farm, during what is called the **NEOLITHIC PERIOD** (the New Stone Age). The most obvious mark they left on the Irish landscape, however, is in the way they buried their dead. The astonishing underground passage graves of **NEWGRANGE, KNOWTH AND DOWTH** in the **BOYNE VALLEY** (older than Stonehenge, the great pyramids of Egypt and the author's jokes) tell us also that they had a sophisticated knowledge of the skies above them. An opening in the roof of the Newgrange burial mound (or tumulus) is perfectly aligned to sunrise on the **WINTER SOLSTICE** (21 December) every year.

THE CÉIDE FIELDS

The hunter-gatherers also left us with some evidence of how they farmed in a place called the Céide Fields in north Mayo. The remnants of houses and burial places there date from around 3000 BC. The Neolithic farmers had cut down trees to create fields for cultivation but, at some point, they abandoned their settlement, which then slowly turned into a bog.

SUPERHEROES

. . . .

Much of what we *think* we know about these Irish Bronze and Iron Age people comes from the ancient legends of the Fianna and the Red Branch Knights. These are tales of the mighty warriors Fionn MacCumhaill (Finn McCool) and Cúchulainn, and lots of superhero types with cool names like Laery the Victorious, Keltar of the Battles and Niall of the Nine Hostages. There's not a lot about farming in these legends, other than some cattle rustling, so you sometimes wonder who fed these ancient Irish ninjas?

ALL THAT GLITTERS

Later, in the **BRONZE AGE** (c. 2500 BC–500 BC) and **IRON AGE** (c. 500 BC–AD 400), our ancient ancestors (usually called **CELTS** or Milesians) began working with metals, including gold. The skills they learned produced some of the wonderful treasures – including torcs (twisted gold necklaces) and lunulas (collars made of thin sheets of gold) – now stored in the National Museum in Kildare Street in Dublin.

NEWGRANGE

When our ancient ancestors buried their dead, they sometimes did it in style. In the case of Newgrange, they had to haul huge boulders over a long distance to build a Neolithic PASSAGE GRAVE. Some people think it was more of an ancient temple than a tomb. The Newgrange tumulus is a large circular mound near a bend in the River Boyne. The tomb, in the form of a CAIRN (which is a word for a pile of stones) was built around 3200 BC. It has a crescent-shaped wall of quartz stones and is surrounded by standing stones placed at irregular intervals. On 21 December every year, the sun should come pouring in through a 'roof box' hole in the top of the cairn and light up the chamber inside. But that all depends on our traditional Irish clouds, doesn't it?

ROOF BOX: This lets the sun into the passage and inner chamber on the shortest day of the year, 21 December, the day of the winter solstice. It is positioned perfectly. Our ancient ancestors knew exactly what they were doing.

ENTRANCE STONE: This stands in front of the entrance to the tomb and is decorated with circles, spirals, chevrons and arcs, a style we think of as 'Celtic' art.

STANDING STONES: Also known as kerbstones, 97 of these ring the cairn at irregular intervals. It would have taken a lot of muscle power to get them there so they must have some religious meaning. Why would you bother otherwise?

AURORA BOREALIS: The famous northern lights were clearly visible over Newgrange on the night of 20 December 2015. Is that tied in to the meaning of the site or just an interesting coincidence?

INNER CHAMBER: In 1967 an archaeologist realised that this room was beautifully lit up by the rising sun on 21 December. The builders of Newgrange may have been sun-worshippers. If so, because this was cloudy old Ireland, they wouldn't have seen much of their god.

HOME OF THE GODS? We aren't the only people to be curious about Brú na Bóinne (Palace of the Boyne). In the past, Newgrange and the nearby Knowth and Dowth mounds were thought to have been the abode of the Tuatha Dé Danann (the 'tribe of the gods') of ancient Irish mythology.

PASSAGE: This measures 19 metres and leads to the inner chamber.

WHAT'S IT ALL ABOUT? Is it just a tomb? Is it a primitive observatory for studying the heavens? Is it an ancient temple? Your guess is as good as anybody's! It certainly is a major tourist attraction, with over 200,000 visitors a year.

EARLY CHRISTIAN IRELAND

The Celts didn't just have a single god. They worshipped deities like Lug, from whom we get the Irish word 'LUGHNASA' meaning August, and Badb, the goddess of war, who adopted the form of a crow. But it took less than a century for Ireland to embrace the new Christian religion. Within a few decades we went from being a land where Balor the one-eyed god could kill you by looking at you crossways to becoming the 'ISLAND OF SAINTS AND SCHOLARS'.

ST PATRICK

It is thought that the first Irish Christians were probably slaves, captured in Britain and brought to Ireland. One of them certainly was. His Latin name was **PATRICIUS**, but we know him better as Patrick. He was enslaved in the early 5th century, when he was 16 years old. He was taken by Irish pirates, escaped back to Britain after six years, became a priest and then returned to Ireland in 432 to make Christians of us.

MISSIONARIES

During the **DARK AGES** in Europe, after the fall of the Roman Empire, many Irish monks and scholars travelled to the continent and established monasteries there. Among these were the 7th-century bishop St Killian, who was beheaded on the orders of an angry German duchess (he said her marriage was illegal), and the 9th-century philosopher Johannes Scotus Eriugena, who later featured on the old Irish £5 note.

MONKS

Thanks to Patrick, it didn't take long for Christianity to take root and for a number of monasteries to be established around the country. Small towns and settlements often grew up beside the most famous monasteries, places like Clonmacnoise (founded by St Ciaran in the 6th century) or Kells (founded by St Colmcille, who also established a monastery on the Scottish island of Iona). Monks in both of these **MONASTIC SETTLEMENTS** completed the famous **BOOK OF KELLS**, a beautifully illustrated manuscript of the gospels.

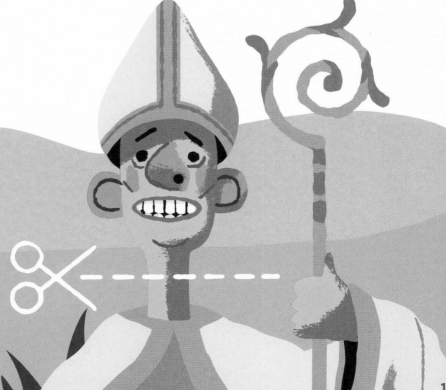

THE VIKINGS IN IRELAND

In the year 795, a monk on the island of Rathlin, off the coast of Antrim, looked out to sea and spotted something odd on the horizon. As it got closer, he realised it was a boat. Because the monks weren't expecting guests, he probably wondered who it was. He didn't have to wait long to find out, and he may not have survived the experience, because the first Vikings were about to land from their speedy LONGBOATS in search of gold, plunder, slaves and ransom.

These Vikings (a Norse word for 'pirates') came from Norway in small but terrifyingly efficient groups. Gradually their attacks became more organised, and the number of Viking ships and sailors increased. Some Norse fleets carried more than 1,000 warriors by the time of the Norse chieftain Ivar the Boneless (don't ask – no one knows how he got his name) in the mid-9th century.

GIVE US YOUR GOLD!

The favourite targets of these lethal Scandinavian tourists were rich Irish monasteries. They often sailed up rivers like the Boyne and Liffey to attack them. Sometimes they would fight among themselves – the Danes (another Viking people) and the Norse were not especially fond of each other. Sometimes they would take sides – if the money was right – in the many wars fought between Irish clan chieftains. This was all long before local rivalries were catered for by the All-Ireland football and hurling championships.

BRIAN BORU

Brian Boru was a very powerful High King at the time of the Viking invasions. He is best known for taking part in the **BATTLE OF CLONTARF**. This battle is known for ridding Ireland of the Vikings but, in fact, different groups of Vikings were fighting on both sides in the battle. Brian Boru was already in his seventies when he led his forces at Clontarf, which was very old for those times. Sadly, although he won the battle, he was one of the casualties that day. Because most Vikings fought on the losing side of the battle, their numbers soon dwindled.

DID THE VIKINGS WEAR HORNS IN THEIR HELMETS?

We often think that a Viking isn't really a Viking unless he's wearing a horned helmet and a ferocious grimace. Except that their headgear didn't have horns. We can blame the German composer Richard Wagner for this myth. In one of his operas the Viking characters were given horned helmets to make them look fiercer. When you think about it, it actually makes sense. How can you wave an axe properly with horns or antlers sticking out of your helmet?

WHAT DID THE VIKINGS EVER DO FOR US?

We have at least one thing to thank these cut-throat, axe-waving pirates for: most of our modern cities. Have you ever wondered why so many big Irish towns tend to be on the coast? It wasn't because we were keen on fish or liked swimming in salt water. It's because these **PORT CITIES** were established by Viking raiders who wanted to stay close to their work (stealing Irish gold) during the long winter months. So, the Vikings gave us Dubhlinn, Weisfjord and Vadfrefjord. What? Never heard of them? Try Dublin, Wexford and Waterford. They were originally ports for the Vikings to moor their longboats for the winter, so the poor lads didn't have such a long commute (obviously, if you are a monastery raider you can't work remotely). Gradually the Vikings began to settle in Ireland – they became known as **OSTMEN** – and develop our large coastal towns.

THE COMING OF THE NORMANS

Ireland in the 12th century was not the place to be if you wanted a quiet life. Rival kings and chieftains were apt to go to war before breakfast, change sides before lunch and slaughter their rivals (along with quite a few peaceful farmers) before settling down to a good evening feast.

Dermot MacMurrough, king of Leinster, was one of the most merciless of a pretty ruthless lot. In 1141 he defeated his rivals in battle and killed or blinded 17 of them to ensure they didn't cause him any further trouble. In 1153, he picked a fight with his great rival Tiernan O'Rourke of BREFFNI (which was the old name for Cavan and Leitrim) and kidnapped O'Rourke's wife, Dervorgilla. However, she might not have been that reluctant to be abducted as she brought all her furniture with her.

STRONGBOW

It took O'Rourke 15 years to get his revenge. In 1166 he invaded Leinster and forced MacMurrough to flee. Although by that time he was not far off today's pension age, instead of retiring and taking up a useful hobby, MacMurrough was determined to get his throne back. He sought the help of Henry II, the king of England. Henry helped him to retake his kingdom by offering some of his top knights. The most prominent of these was Richard fitz Gilbert de Clare, Earl of Pembroke (in west Wales), also known as Strongbow. In return for military aid, Dermot promised Strongbow the hand of his daughter Aoife in marriage and the kingdom of Leinster when he died.

MACMURROUGH RETURNS WITH HIS NORMAN MATES

A small group of Norman invaders arrived in Ireland in 1169. The Normans originally came from France and conquered England and Wales in 1066. The forces of the Irish chieftains were no match for these armour-clad knights and the well-aimed arrows of their archers, and Wexford was quickly taken. In 1170, Strongbow landed with a larger force, captured Waterford and Dublin and took military control of Dermot's old kingdom. When Dermot died the following year, Strongbow became king of Leinster. In 1171, Henry II arrived with a large force of his own – just in case Strongbow might be getting any big ideas about trying to seize the English throne after his success in Ireland. Henry declared himself **LORD OF IRELAND**. He then accepted the (not very sincere) loyalty of Norman and Gaelic lords alike. The Irish chieftains had no intention of actually obeying King Henry if they could get away with it, but he had a large army (up to 5,000 men) so they weren't taking any chances.

THE RIGHT TO INVADE IRELAND

For centuries MacMurrough has been known in Irish as Diarmait na nGall (Dermot of the Foreigners) because he brought the Normans to Ireland, but if anyone is to blame for the first British 'invasion' of Ireland, it was the only English-born pope, Adrian IV. In 1155, he granted the English king the right to invade Ireland. MacMurrough just gave Henry II a half-decent excuse. He, or one of his successors, probably would have got around to us sooner or later. But it's always good to have a pantomime villain to blame. So, boo, hiss, Dermot MacMurrough.

DERVORGILLA O'ROURKE

We tend to blame Dermot MacMurrough for inviting the Norman invaders to Ireland. We should take a closer look at the incident that resulted in his exile in the first place: the 'kidnapping' of Dervorgilla, wife of Tiernan O'Rourke of Breffni.

Dervorgilla was born in 1108 , daughter of the king of Meath. She was 20 years old when her father arranged her marriage to Tiernan O'Rourke, chieftain of the neighbouring Breffni. Then, in 1152, Dermot MacMurrough, king of Leinster, showed up and carried her off. This is where things get spotty and confusing and why history is full of wonderful rows and differences of opinion.

Some historians think MacMurrough removed her from Breffni by prior arrangement ... with Dervorgilla herself, because the two were madly in love. Others believe that MacMurrough did abduct her, just to annoy his enemy Tiernan O'Rourke. Still more experts reckon that Dervorgilla was removed from Breffni to get her out of harm's way because a war was raging in which her husband was involved. This theory suggests that she was back with Tiernan, no harm done, within a year. But then there's that bit about her taking her furniture and cattle with her when Dermot came calling. This suggests that she thought she was going (willingly) on a long trip.

CATHAL CROBHDEARG O'CONNOR

There is a type of person (you may know one or two) who always seems to know which way the wind is blowing. This means they are never taken by surprise. Cathal Crobhdearg (Red Claw) O'Connor – king of Connacht (on and off) from 1198 to the time of his death in 1224 – was one of those people. He was also one of at least 25 children. His father, Turlough, went through five wives and died in the arms of his sixth. He must have loved weddings.

Cathal Crobhdearg came to power at a time when the Normans were starting to eye Connacht and say to themselves, 'I'd like a bit of that.' Then his kingdom was taken from him by his own nephew, also called Cathal O'Connor (his nickname was Cathal Carrach, or Cathal of the Scabs, so he probably didn't have great skin). That didn't matter much after a while because Uncle Cathal killed him and regained the throne of Connacht in 1202, hanging on to it for the next 22

years, constantly changing sides at the first sign of trouble. When a war broke out he was happy to team up with anyone, including the Normans, who would help him keep his lands. According to accounts at the time, he also holds the world record for killing, blinding and mutilating his opponents. That's the kind of thing you had to do back in the 13th century to stay ahead of the game – and Cathal Crobhdearg had a talent for it.

A MEDIEVAL STONE CASTLE

TOWER: These were built into the walls, often at the corners of the castle. They were taller than the walls and offered a better view of any Irish foolish enough to attack.

DRAWBRIDGE: This bridge across the moat could be raised or lowered when needed.

Soon after their invasion, the Normans began to build the same sort of stone castles they had already constructed in England and Wales. One of the best examples is the home of the de Lacys in Trim, County Meath. It overlooks the River Boyne – a reliable source of nearby water was always important. The stone castle was a superior form of protection to a wooden castle and often included a surrounding moat filled with water. A number of high towers were built into the surrounding walls. A drawbridge over the moat led to a gate called a portcullis. Inside the walls were lots of buildings, but the most important one was the keep, where the Norman lords' and ladies' private rooms were.

TRIM CASTLE: It took the de Lacys 30 years to build this castle in the 12th century. Today it's run by the Office of Public Works as a monument of national importance.

KEEP: This building inside the castle walls housed the sleeping and eating accommodation of the lord and lady of the castle, along with their servants and soldiers.

WALL: Known as the 'curtain wall', this surrounded and protected the central keep.

BRAVEHEART: Some of the Mel Gibson film about William Wallace of Scotland was filmed in Trim Castle in 1994. The castle doubled for the cities of both London and York.

MOAT: This surrounded the castle and could be filled with water. No, there weren't any crocodiles swimming in it for added protection. Good idea, though! Go to the top of the class.

THE MIDDLE AGES

For the next four hundred years, the size of the English colony in Ireland kept changing. A COLONY is where a group of people from one country build a settlement in someone else's. The size of the colony in Ireland depended on the interest of the reigning English MONARCH (another name for ruler) or the talent of the Gaelic chieftains for making trouble. Many of the new Norman settlers married into Gaelic families, learned to speak Irish, adopted Irish customs, formed alliances with Gaelic chieftains and became 'more Irish than the Irish themselves'.

An bhfuil cead agam dul go dtí an leithreas?

THE STATUTES OF KILKENNY

The English king Edward III took a great interest in his Irish colony, though not a friendly one. During his reign, in 1366, a set of laws known as the Statutes of Kilkenny was introduced. These were meant to prevent his ANGLO-NORMAN subjects from mixing or marrying with the rowdy native Irish. The Anglo-Normans were to stop speaking Irish, obey English laws only and stop playing Irish sports like 'horlings'. You can probably guess what 'horlings' was, but it was only a coincidence that they went to Kilkenny to ban it.

THE PALE

At times the land controlled by the Normans shrank in size all the way back to an area known as the Pale (meaning 'fence'), which stretched from south of Dublin as far as Dundalk to the north and inland to parts of northern Kildare. At times like these the inhabitants of the Pale thought of anyone living 'BEYOND THE PALE' as dangerous savages.

THE BLACK DEATH

Far worse, however, than anything the native Irish could do to those within the Pale was the the bubonic plague, also known as the Black Death. It arrived in Ireland in 1348, carried by flea-infested rats (as if rats weren't bad enough on their own). Victims came out in boils, vomited blood and died within days. The effect on the Anglo-Norman population was worse than on the 'Old Irish' because many of the Anglo-Normans lived in towns, where the plague spread far more easily. By the time the Black Death had run its course in Ireland, it had claimed at least one-third of the population.

HOW TO BECOME A MEDIEVAL IRISH CHIEFTAIN
· · · · · · · · · · · ·

Well, it's obvious, innit? The eldest son of the dead chieftain takes over. Eh ... not so fast!
In fact, under the ancient Irish Brehon laws, when a clan chieftain died, any male within four generations could inherit. It was an invitation for the killing, blinding and maiming to start until one sighted survivor won out. Take Connacht for example. Between 1274 and 1315, the province had 13 kings – an average of almost one every three years – 9 of which were murdered by their brothers or cousins. Whatever happened to brotherly love?

NORMAN HOSPITALITY?

In 1305 Norman lord Peter de Bermingham invited 30 of his wild O'Connor neighbours to a banquet. Foolishly, they accepted his invitation without checking the small print. He then had them murdered before the starters arrived. They were all decapitated and their heads were passed on to the authorities to claim a reward.

WHAT DID THE NORMANS EVER DO FOR US?

They gave us some nice stone castles – the castles at Trim and Carrickfergus get loads of tourists every year – and people with the word 'fitz' or 'de' in their names, like Fitzgerald or de Courcy (but not de Valera, our future Taoiseach and president – his name was Spanish).

IRELAND UNDER THE TUDORS

Apart from occasional hostilities in the Aviva Stadium, we get on really well with Wales ... now! But, just as the invading Normans came from Wales, so did the original members of the Tudor family. They became monarchs of England in the late 15th century and left their mark here in all sorts of unpleasant ways.

The second Tudor king, Henry VIII, was a great believer in marriage, so much so that he had six wives. But in 1534, when he couldn't persuade the pope to end his first marriage, he had a bit of a tantrum. He made himself head of his own church and insisted that his subjects follow him as a church leader as well as a king. This was called the REFORMATION. We Irish weren't terribly keen on Henry's Reformation, especially when he began to close Catholic monasteries and distribute the land to his followers.

THE REBELLION OF SILKEN THOMAS

For decades, members of the powerful FitzGerald family, the earls of Kildare, were LORDS DEPUTY, which meant they ran the country on behalf of the king. The 9th Earl of Kildare, Gerald FitzGerald, took over in 1513. For the next 20 years he was in and out of favour with Henry VIII. In 1533 Fitzgerald was summoned to London and left his headstrong son, Thomas, in his place as Lord Deputy. The 21-year-old, known as 'Silken' Thomas because of his love of fine clothing, was taken in by a false rumour that his father had been executed. He rebelled against Henry VIII but, despite some early successes, was defeated and, along with his six uncles, was beheaded. (Chopping people's heads off was one of Henry VIII's hobbies. He had two of his six wives beheaded.)

DID THE BATTLE OF KINSALE TAKE PLACE IN 1601 OR 1602?

. . . .

The answer is 'Yes'!

This is not quite as contradictory as it sounds. For centuries, time had been measured by an old Roman system called the Julian calendar, called after the Roman emperor Julius Caesar. Then, in 1582, Pope Gregory XIII came up with an alternative, the Gregorian calendar, where everything shifted forward by ten days or so. Naturally enough, the Protestant English, not being big fans of the pope, stuck with Caesar's version. So, they fought their Battle of Kinsale on Christmas Eve 1601, while the Irish fought *their* Battle of Kinsale on 3 January 1602!

Santa brought the English a nice (for them) Christmas present – victory.

THE TWO HUGHS

The most powerful Gaelic chieftains of the 16th century were Hugh O'Neill and 'Red' Hugh O'Donnell (because he had red hair, of course!). They were also the earls of Tyrone and of Tyrconnell (an old name for Donegal), as their ancestors had accepted English titles during the reign of Henry VIII. However, when Queen Elizabeth I (Henry VIII's daughter) tried to colonise more of Ireland, both men rebelled and the NINE YEARS WAR (1594–1603) began. After winning a number of battles, the two Hughs were finally defeated at the BATTLE OF KINSALE in 1601. Spain, which was also at war with England, offered support but when its forces landed in County Cork – not much use to O'Neill and O'Donnell in Ulster, at the other end of the country – they were surrounded by a British army. O'Neill and O'Donnell went on a long trek south to come to the rescue and surrounded the British. Rather than starve the enemy out, O'Donnell insisted on an attack. It failed, and after the defeat of the Irish, the Spaniards surrendered. The two Hughs both fled to Spain.

CROMWELL IN IRELAND

After the defeat at Kinsale, the lands of O'Neill, O'Donnell and their Ulster allies were seized for the new king of England, James Stuart (James I), and 'planted' with Scottish and English Protestant settlers in the ULSTER PLANTATION. The planters replaced the original landowners.

Resentment boiled over when the Ulster Catholics tried to take back their lands in a rebellion that led to a number of horrible massacres of Protestants. The worst one took place in Portadown in November 1641, where more than 100 men, women and children were murdered. This slaughter was recorded (and sometimes exaggerated) in a series of accounts known as the 1641 DEPOSITIONS, which are held in Trinity College, Dublin.

CROMWELL ARRIVES

Meanwhile, in England, a row broke out between the new king, Charles I, and the leader of the English parliament, Oliver Cromwell. Cromwell wanted the people (through the parliament) to have more say in how their tax money was spent. His supporters were called ROUNDHEADS (because they wore their hair short). The king's supporters were the ROYALISTS. Civil war broke out between the Roundheads and Royalists. This ended when Cromwell had Charles I beheaded in 1649. Then Cromwell turned his attention to Ireland, where the Irish supporters of the king (the CONFEDERACY) were trying to take control. He arrived in Ireland in 1649 with an army of 12,000 men.

DROGHEDA

One of the first places to oppose Cromwell's forces was the walled town of Drogheda in County Louth. Cromwell offered to spare the Confederate and Royalist soldiers if they surrendered. They refused, and the town was attacked in September 1649 and fell to Cromwell's soldiers. Because they had refused to surrender when given the chance, the defenders of the town could now be executed. Cromwell ordered that no mercy was to be shown to 'these barbarous wretches', and around 2,500 Confederacy troops were slaughtered, along with an estimated 800 townspeople. Cromwell, who also saw himself as revenging the 1641 massacres, hoped that word of the slaughter would spread and persuade other Confederacy-held towns to surrender without a fight. The same thing happened a few weeks later in the town of Wexford, where another 2,000 people were killed.

THE 'IRISH' CROMWELL VS. THE 'ENGLISH' CROMWELL

· · · · · · · · · · · · · ·

In England, there is a statue of him in Westminster. In Ireland, a monument to Oliver Cromwell would rapidly be vandalised. To the average English person, Oliver Cromwell is the father of their democracy. To the Irish, he's a cruel tyrant who murdered thousands of our 17th-century ancestors. The truth, of course, is that he was both. He reduced the power of the English monarchy while also behaving ruthlessly in his conquest of Ireland.

OLIVER CROMWELL 1599 1658

'TO HELL OR TO CONNACHT'

Cromwell's brutal campaign in Ireland was also intended to pay for itself by taking land from the defeated Irish, most of whom were Catholics. This led to the Cromwellian plantation, which sent many Irish landowners, as Cromwell put it himself, 'to hell or to Connacht' and handed over huge areas of good Irish land to Cromwell's officers (many of whom later sold it on to English settlers). This meant that most Irish land would be owned by Protestants. They would become known as the Protestant 'ASCENDANCY', which means 'ruling class'.

KING BILLY AND KING JAMES

In 1685 England got what most of its people didn't want: a Catholic king, James II. Within three years he had lost his throne to his son-in-law, William, Prince of Orange, a Dutch Protestant nobleman married to James's daughter Mary. (William later became known as King Billy.) James asked for help from the great French king Louis XIV and, with a group of French troops, arrived in Ireland in 1689 to regain his throne via the 'back door'. Not to be outdone, William landed in Ireland himself with a force of Dutch and English troops.

THE BATTLE OF THE BOYNE

James suffered his first major defeat at the Battle of the Boyne, near Drogheda, in 1690. William's forces were almost double the size of James's army. How could they lose with 24,000 troops to the 12,000 of the French and Irish army? The answer is they couldn't. They used this advantage to overpower James's army on 12 July 1690. William's victory at the Boyne allowed him to take nearby Dublin.

THE BATTLE OF AUGHRIM

The Battle of the Boyne was the last defeat of King James II in Ireland, but only because he fled the country afterwards and left his forces to fend for themselves. They did quite well at the siege of Limerick (a SIEGE is where a town is surrounded and the people are starved into surrender), where the Irish and French won. But they then lost the bloodiest battle ever fought on Irish soil: the Battle of Aughrim in 1691. Around 4,000 JACOBITES, the supporters of King James, were killed and left on the Galway fields. William's supporters, called WILLIAMITES, lost about half that number.

WHOSE SIDE WAS THE POPE ON?

You'd think the pope would have been on the side of the English Catholic King James II. Then why were church bells in the Vatican rung in celebration when news of his defeat at the Boyne reached Rome? This was because the battle was part of a wider European war in which the pope was on the opposite side to King Louis XIV of France, who supported King James II. So, that meant the pope was a supporter of King Billy!

THE PENAL LAWS

Finally, the Jacobites and Williamites signed a treaty that ended the war. One of the main points of this agreement was that Catholics would be allowed to practise their religion freely. It wasn't long, however, before this promise was broken by a series of anti-Catholic laws that said Catholics couldn't own guns, or a horse worth more than £5, or educate their children abroad, or or be elected to the House of Commons, one of the two houses of parliament. (The other was the House of Lords, whose members were appointed by the monarch.). These and other so-called 'Penal Laws' left Protestants in charge in Ireland for almost two centuries.

A PALLADIAN MANSION

One of Ireland's most famous mansions was owned by William Conolly, an extremely rich man and member of the Protestant Ascendancy. Conolly was the Speaker of the Irish House of Commons. This meant that he made sure the members behaved themselves. His country home, Castletown House in Celbridge, County Kildare, is built in the Palladian style, named after the 16th-century Italian architect Andrea Palladio, who borrowed a lot of ideas from the ancient Greeks and Romans. These, and many more besides, were the 'BIG HOUSE' homes of rich Irish landowners – the ARISTOCRATS.

FOUR-POSTERS: These are beds with four wooden uprights covered with canopies and often surrounded by curtains. You would only find them in the upstairs bedrooms.

WHITE HOUSE: Irish Palladian mansions influenced the Irish architect James Hoban (who was from Kilkenny) in his design of the White House in Washington DC.

HA-HA: Despite the name, this is no laughing matter: it's a sunken fence or wall built to create two tiers in a sloping lawn. This kept livestock out but allowed an uninterrupted view of smooth green grass from the Big House.

WINDOWS: There were a lot of these in a Palladian mansion – more than a hundred in Castletown House, for example. They were wooden sash windows with shutters and a system of weights to make them easier to open and close.

CHANDELIERS: These hung from the ceiling and used glass crystal prisms to help spread light. The name comes from the French word *chandelle*, meaning 'candle', because that's what they used before electricity.

FAMILY PORTRAITS: Most Big Houses had paintings of the lords and ladies of the manor on their walls. You'd have to check the attic for portraits of the family 'black sheep'.

DUMB WAITER: This has nothing to do with the intelligence of the staff. It is a lift operated by a pulley system for transporting food and drink up to a dining room from a kitchen 'below stairs'.

KITCHENS: These were often vast in a Big House. The kitchens in Strokestown House have a sort of balcony (called a gallery) so the lady of the house could toss notes down to the cook complaining about the soup or demanding something nice for dessert.

MAZE: There is no maze in Castletown House, but there is one in Russborough House in Wicklow. Bring a flare gun or activate the GPS on Mum's mobile phone in case you get lost (actually, you don't need to – you can buy a map).

THE UNITED IRISHMEN

By the late 1700s, Britain had colonies all around the world, including America. Many Americans wanted independence from Britain. They revolted against the English monarch in the AMERICAN WAR OF INDEPENDENCE in 1775. Around the same time, a revolution was taking place in France against their own monarch. These two revolutions encouraged some Irish to fight for independence.

THE VOLUNTEERS

In 1778, a number of Irish rebels formed an armed group called the Volunteers. It had about 100,000 members. When the well-armed Volunteers demanded an independent Irish parliament in Dublin, the British government had little choice but to give in. This came about in 1782, and the most impressive person in the new independent parliament was the great Irish politician Henry Grattan, a supporter of EMANCIPATION (freedom) for Catholics from the Penal Laws. It is often called 'GRATTAN'S PARLIAMENT' after him.

THE UNITED IRISHMEN

But for some people, this Irish parliament in College Green in Dublin was not enough. It was a Protestant assembly of landowners and noblemen. They wanted what France had achieved in its famous revolution of 1789: a republic, a nation no longer ruled by a king and a wealthy landowning aristocracy. They formed an organisation, led by a young Protestant named Wolfe Tone, called the United Irishmen. The United Irishmen began to plan a rebellion against British rule. The United Irishmen included many Ulster Protestants who supported Catholic rights, as well as Catholic rebels. One of its Dublin leaders was the aristocrat Lord Edward FitzGerald.

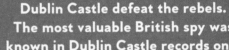

WHO WAS JW?

Spies and informers within the ranks of the United Irishmen helped Dublin Castle defeat the rebels. The most valuable British spy was known in Dublin Castle records only as 'JW'. He was exposed many years later as Leonard McNally, a barrister who defended many 1798 rebels in the trials that ended their lives. No one got suspicious, even though he didn't win a single case. He was paid £300 a year for his work, worth about €30,000 today. Spying and treachery was a rewarding profession. Let's hear more of those boos and hisses please!

THE 1798 REBELLION

When the rebellion took place in 1798, the Irishmen were anything but united. Risings happened in a disorganised way in different parts of the country. Plans for the uprising went wrong because DUBLIN CASTLE, the seat of English power in Ireland, was well-informed about them through their network of spies. Lord Edward FitzGerald was killed as he was being arrested in Dublin, ending any hope of a successful rising in the capital city. Separate battles in Wexford and Antrim were quickly defeated. The arrival of a small French force in Mayo in August might have rekindled the rebellion, but the French were rapidly seen off as well. When he attempted to land in Donegal with yet another French force, Wolfe Tone was captured and ended his own life before he could be executed.

THE ACT OF UNION

One of the results of the 1798 rebellion was a decision by the British government to pass the 1801 Act of Union. This meant there would be no Irish parliament any more, and Irish members would travel to London instead and vote at Westminster. Because the old Irish parliament was entirely Protestant, Dublin Castle reckoned that most Catholics would be happy to see it abolished, especially if CATHOLIC EMANCIPATION – the election of Catholic Members of Parliament (MPs) – was offered at the same time. This was one of the reasons why many Catholics actually supported the Act of Union.

AFTER THE ACT OF UNION

Ireland was now part of the United Kingdom of Great Britain and Ireland and entitled to 100 Irish members in the English parliament. This may sound like a lot, but in 1800 Ireland made up a third of the total population of the two islands (4 million out of 12 million) and there were 658 members in the enlarged House of Commons. Catholic Emancipation didn't happen in the end because the king, George III, was opposed to the idea. This led to Catholics quickly turning against the Act of Union.

ROBERT EMMET'S REBELLION

Robert Emmet was a young idealistic rebel, opposed to the Act of Union, who gathered a small force and took to the streets of Dublin on 23 July 1803. His attempted rebellion quickly fell apart because it had little support from outside the city. Emmet fled but was captured after a month and put on trial for his life. After he was found guilty, he made a famous speech from the dock that would inspire future generations of Irish rebels. In the speech he declared that he didn't want his tombstone to be engraved until Ireland was free. 'Let no man write my epitaph,' he told the court. 'When my country takes her place among the nations of the earth, then, and not till then, let my epitaph be written.' He was hanged and beheaded in Dublin's Thomas Street the day after his conviction.

JOINING THE 'CLUB'

The 100 Irish MPs who now travelled to Westminster for work were really joining a sort posh club with some strange rules. For a start, parliament didn't meet very often so they had plenty of leisure time. MPs were chosen by a small number of wealthy people. One MP only had to secure four votes to get elected! Political parties had nicknames (Tory, Whig) rather than real ones. When you were slagging off another MP you had to call him 'my honourable friend', even though you probably didn't believe he was honourable and he certainly wasn't your friend. On top of all that, if you said something another MP considered personally insulting ('cur', 'cad' and 'bounder' were the favourite terms of abuse back then) he could challenge you to a duel – back to back, pistols in hand, walk ten paces, turn, fire. That sort of duel.

CATHOLIC EMANCIPATION

Because the British government broke their promise to introduce Catholic Emancipation, Irish Catholics never really supported the newly created UNITED KINGDOM OF GREAT BRITAIN AND IRELAND. Catholics could not become members of parliament and most of the land of Ireland was in the hands of Protestant landlords. So, Catholics were shut out from political and economic life by the Protestant Ascendancy.

A number of minor rebellions against high rents and evictions took place in different parts of the country, started by illegal secret societies with exotic names like WHITEBOYS, RIBBONMEN, ROCKITES, CARAVATS and TERRY-ALTS. But the main national political organisation, the CATHOLIC ASSOCIATION, was more concerned with winning CATHOLIC 'RELIEF' – the right to take seats in the Westminster parliament.

DANIEL O'CONNELL

The leader of the Catholic Association was Daniel O'Connell. He had been against the Act of Union and was a thorn in the side of Dublin Castle and of ascendancy Protestants who wanted to keep the link with Britain. They were called UNIONISTS because they believed in the 'union' of Britain and Ireland. The campaign for emancipation was funded by the 'CATHOLIC RENT', a monthly payment of a penny by members of the association. This connected ordinary members more closely to the organisation. O'Connell was a proud Kerryman and a barrister who defended other Irish nationalists in court. He was a great believer in non-violent politics. He once said that freedom for Ireland was 'not worth shedding a single drop of blood'.

O'CONNELL BECOMES AN MP

The real breakthrough for the Catholic Association came in 1828 when a seat in the House of Commons became vacant in County Clare. Although he was not allowed to take a seat in parliament because he was a Catholic, O'Connell stood for election and won. This resulted in a crisis for the British government, which the Catholic Association had wanted all along. The government was afraid of causing a rebellion in Ireland if O'Connell was not allowed to take his seat. In 1829, the prime minister, the Duke of Wellington, reluctantly agreed to introduce a new law to grant Catholic Emancipation, and Daniel O'Connell became Member of Parliament for County Clare.

THE O'CONNELL– D'ESTERRE DUEL

· · · · · · · · · · · · · · · · · · · ·

After O'Connell insulted the men who ran the city of Dublin (Dublin Corporation) in 1815, one of its members, John d'Esterre, decided to be really offended and challenged O'Connell to a duel. This wasn't entirely d'Esterre's idea – he had been put up to it by fellow members of the corporation. They figured that if O'Connell refused to fight he would be labelled as a coward, and if he accepted the challenge he would be killed by d'Esterre, who was a deadly shot. However, the duel did not go according to plan. D'Esterre fired first and missed. O'Connell aimed to wound but his successful shot resulted in the death of his opponent two days later.

WILLIAM ROWAN HAMILTON

Ireland has produced some excellent mathematicians and graffiti artists. On 16 October 1843, William Rowan Hamilton, professor of astronomy at Trinity College Dublin, became a bit of both. On that day, he was walking along the banks of the Royal Canal with his wife. If they were having a conversation, then he wasn't listening to her side of it because he was thinking about a mathematical theory that had just popped into his head. It was to do with quaternions. (No, I haven't a clue either!) Hamilton was afraid he might forget the theory before he could get home and write it down. So, as they approached Broom Bridge, near Cabra in north Dublin, he took out a knife, which must have worried his wife a bit. However, he used the knife to carve a mathematical equation on the bridge. It looked like this ...

$$i^2 = j^2 = k^2 = ijk = -1$$

I don't understand it either. It might as well be Klingon or Parseltongue. But it made him very famous.

SPOTLIGHT ON
BIDDY EARLY

Was Biddy Early a herbalist or was she an evil witch? She was born in 1798, buried three husbands, married a man in his 30s when she was 70, defied the priests of County Clare, was found not guilty of witchcraft and looked after the aches and pains of thousands of people and their animals without asking for payment (though she welcomed donations).

Biddy lived all her life in County Clare and in her youth was said to 'talk to the fairies'. She probably learned all her herbal recipes, which she used

to cure people, from her mother, and her reputation spread quickly. Grateful 'patients' would often repay her with strong drink, usually illegal *poitín* made in secret and consisting of almost pure alcohol. So, her house, as well as being a surgery and dispensary, became a centre where local people often came to polish off her supply of spirits (alcoholic, not ghostly).

Because of her profession and her methods, she was not popular with the Roman Catholic clergy of Feakle and Dromore in County Clare. In 1865,

she was put on trial for witchcraft under a 300-year-old law. The charges were thrown out when the witnesses who were supposed to testify against her changed their minds. Biddy never made any money from her caring work and, sadly, she died in poverty in 1874. That would never have happened to a real witch, now would it?

THE REPEAL CAMPAIGN

After the success of the Catholic Emancipation campaign, O'Connell, by now known as 'THE LIBERATOR' to his supporters, became the leader of a group of about 50 Irish Catholic MPs in the House of Commons. They formed an alliance with the governing WHIGS, one of the two big parties in the House of Commons at that time, and set about achieving reforms that would benefit Ireland.

In 1841 the Whigs were defeated by the Conservative (Tory) party, led by O'Connell's deadly rival Sir Robert Peel (they had come close to duelling once). The Irish party knew they weren't going to get anything out of the Tories, so they decided to make a big effort to end the union between Britain and Ireland – in other words, to repeal the Act of Union. The REPEAL ASSOCIATION was formed, and in 1843 a series of public meetings was organised around the country – O'Connell spoke at many of these. Because of the massive attendances at these gatherings they became known as MONSTER MEETINGS.

THE FAILURE OF REPEAL

The size of these monster meetings, which often took place at historic sites like Tara, worried the Peel government and Irish Protestants who didn't want an independent Irish government where most of the power would be held by Catholics. The final monster meeting of the repeal campaign was due to take place in Clontarf on 7 October 1843. Fearing violence and rebellion if it was allowed to go ahead, the authorities in Dublin Castle banned the meeting. In order to avoid bloodshed, O'Connell, who was opposed to political violence, ordered that the meeting be abandoned. Many of his supporters, including a group of young men within the Repeal Association known as YOUNG IRELAND, were angry and disappointed at what they saw as O'Connell's surrender to Peel.

O'CONNELL'S TRIAL

Robert Peel's government then decided to make an example of O'Connell and the Repeal Association leaders. A number of them were put on trial and jailed for periods of up to a year. These included O'Connell, who was then almost 70 years old and in bad health. A court ordered that the prisoners had not had a fair trial so they were released early. When he got out of jail, O'Connell walked home from the prison without any fuss. However, this was not nearly dramatic enough for his supporters. So he was quietly returned to the prison and 'released' to a huge crowd of followers the next day. They created a great racket as they brought him back to his home in Merrion Square.

THE MONSTER MEETING SOUND SYSTEM

Imagine you are attending the largest of those monster meetings, held at Tara. But you are at the back of the crowd trying to catch Daniel O'Connell's speech. He doesn't have a microphone or a huge sound system, so how do you hear him? Well, the truth is that you don't. Instead, posted at regular intervals through the crowd are Repeal Association officials called 'wardens' with copies of O'Connell's speech. They take their cue from the warden nearest to them and shout out the contents of the speech. So only the first few rows ever actually heard the Liberator himself. You should have got there early, shouldn't you?

THE GREAT FAMINE: THE POTATO BLIGHT

According to the 1841 census, the population of Ireland was 8.2 million. Had it kept growing at the expected rate, by 1851 it would have been close to 9 million. Instead the numbers declined to 6.5 million in 1851. What happened between 1841 and 1851? Where did millions of people go?

The simple answer is that almost half of them died of starvation and disease and the rest emigrated. The reason was an unwelcome visitor in the summer of 1845 called Phytophthora infestans. The dreaded disease of potato blight had arrived in Europe from the Americas. The reason for Ireland's high population before the potato blight was because the diet of people in rural Ireland was based on plentiful supplies of potatoes. People could live on very small pockets of land and survive because of the nutritious 'lumper' variety of potato. Blight killed off almost half of the crop in 1845, and 86 per cent of the normal yield rotted in the ground in 1847. The result was catastrophic for rural Ireland, where most of the country's population lived.

THE FIRST RESPONSE

Robert Peel's government actually got to work very quickly to help the desperate Irish. Supplies of corn were imported from the USA and distributed to the starving. Those worst affected were able to seek shelter in the recently opened workhouses designed to accommodate the poor. Public works projects, such as building walls or roads, were set up to employ people who could then buy (just) enough food to keep them alive. The real problems began when Peel was replaced by a new British prime minister, Lord John Russell, himself an owner of Irish land. Russell's party did not believe in intervening in the tragedy happening in Ireland. Publicly funded works projects were shut down and replaced with soup kitchens. Later, these too were closed. The numbers of starving people trying to get into workhouses simply exploded. These buildings became overcrowded and were overwhelmed by the deadly diseases associated with famine – fever, typhus and cholera. Private charity organisations, often run by members of a religious group THE SOCIETY OF FRIENDS (also called Quakers), struggled to deal with the growing crisis.

THE 1848 REBELLION

In the midst of hundreds of thousands of deaths from starvation and disease, Daniel O'Connell died in 1847. The Young Ireland faction, who had begun to oppose O'Connell within the Repeal Association, had been expelled from the movement. They chose the following year, 1848, to organise a rebellion against British rule. It took place when the population was exhausted from fighting famine. The rebellion was quickly put down and most of the Young Ireland leadership was transported to Australia, which was then a **PRISON COLONY**, where prisoners were sent to work for the rest of their lives

EUROPE AND THE POTATO BLIGHT

Phytophthora infestans did not just affect Ireland. Blight spread right across Europe. Potato yields in Belgium, for example, were down 87 per cent in 1845, an even higher rate than our own. The Netherlands experienced a 71 per cent drop. The big difference was in the impact on the people themselves. Only the Scottish Highlands experienced anything like the catastrophe in Ireland. European countries did not depend on the potato as much as Ireland. For most Irish people, the potato was almost all they had to eat.

SOCIETY of FRIENDS

THE GREAT FAMINE: EVICTIONS AND CLEARANCES

The collapse of the potato crop three times in the mid-1840s would have been bad enough on its own, but it was accompanied by the eviction of hundreds of thousands of starving tenant farmers from the small plots of land they rented from wealthy landlords. Up to half a million people lost their farms between 1845 and 1850. Almost 70,000 families were evicted *after* the worst of the famine itself had passed, between 1849 and 1856.

Widespread estate clearances began when the government under Prime Minister Lord John Russell insisted that 'Irish property must pay for Irish poverty'. That meant that public relief works and the country's workhouses would no longer be supported by British taxes but would have to be paid for by the taxes of Irish property owners. These were mostly landlords on whose estates thousands of Irish tenant farmers were already struggling to survive.

THE FAMINE CLEARANCES

Some Irish landlords lost almost all of their savings in their attempts to help their tenants. Others did little or nothing. But a small number of Irish landowners made matters far worse for the rural poor. They hit on a solution to the problem of the increased amount of money in taxes being demanded of them. If a landlord could clear his estate of tenants by evicting them, and if they then moved to a city like Dublin or left the country altogether, they became someone else's problem, and the landlord could rent the land to someone else. Some landlords even figured it was worth their while to pay tenants to emigrate rather than have them evicted. It cost money to evict because you had to apply to a court to throw out one of your tenants. Why not pay their way to New York instead?

EVICTION!

The number of evictions trebled to 10,000 a year between 1846 and 1848. Clearances (the eviction of more than 40 families at a time) took place on almost 50 estates. These were often accompanied by the destruction of the cottages of the evicted tenants. The evictees were then left to survive in SCALPEENS: lean-tos dug into a ditch on the side of the public road. A Mrs Gerrard, for example, who evicted almost an entire Galway village (Ballinglass near Mountbellew) in 1846, was asked by a reporter for a comment. She replied, 'Thank you, I am well, thriving, and getting fat on the curses of the wretches.' Many of the worst landlords simply replaced their evicted tenants with cattle and sheep who had even fewer rights than their former tenants.

HELP COMES FROM THE CHOCTAWS

The horrors of the famine were publicised in newspapers and magazines all over the world, especially in America. That was how the plight of the Irish people came to the attention of the Native American Choctaw tribe 4,000 miles away. In the 1830s they had been moved from their homes by the US government onto much poorer land. The Choctaws had very little money but they were so appalled when they heard what was happening in Ireland that they managed to collect $170 – a colossal amount of money to them – and sent it to Ireland to buy food for the starving people there. In 2020 the Native American Navajo and Hopi nations were amazed when thousands of dollars came online from Ireland to help them fight coronavirus. They couldn't figure out why Irish people would want to contribute to ease their struggle. They only understood when they read messages left by the Irish donors thanking the Choctaws for their generosity towards our ancestors.

A LOOK ◉ INSIDE
A COFFIN SHIP

For many of the poor and starving Irish who tried to leave the country in order to survive after 1845, it was a case of 'out of the frying pan, into the fire'. Many famine refugees got no further than Britain. Some emigrants headed for Australia but most attempted to get to the USA and Canada. Many of them ended up as passengers on filthy, sub-standard Atlantic vessels that have become known as 'COFFIN SHIPS'. Some were fortunate enough to be able to save the price of the fare, only to find disease, dehydration, hunger and unsanitary conditions on board the ships that were supposed to bring them to the 'NEW WORLD'. Around 20,000 died making the trip in 1847 alone.

OVERCROWDING: Ships bound for Canada had looser regulations than those heading for the USA and often had two or three times more passengers than would have been allowed on a US-bound ship.

THE WORKHOUSE: Often the only alternative to the emigrant ship for the worst off, workhouses were large miserable buildings, set up by the government, where people lived in overcrowded conditions. You would be fed just enough to keep you alive but also stood a good chance of catching a fatal disease.

THE ATLANTIC CROSSING: From ports in Ireland and Britain, this journey could last from six weeks to three months, depending on the weather and the speed of the ship. However, even on reaching north America many ships containing Irish emigrants were required to remain offshore for fear of the spread of disease.

BARQUE: Also called a 'bark' or a 'barc', this was a three- or four-masted sailing ship. Many coffin ships were barques. They were usually built to accommodate around 100 passengers but often carried more than twice that number.

THE *SIR HENRY POTTINGER*: A good example of a coffin ship, this was named after the first governor of Hong Kong. It sailed for Canada with 399 passengers, lost 98 at sea and arrived with 112 more either sick or dying.

FIRST CLASS: Strange as it may seem, many of the Atlantic passenger ships had rooms above deck for wealthy first-class passengers. One of those, Robert Whyte, wrote an account of the hardships of the Irish passengers below deck, *A Voyage to Quebec on an Irish Emigrant Vessel*.

BURIAL AT SEA: If you died in the hold of a coffin ship, your body would simply be thrown overboard.

BELOW DECK: This is where most of the Irish were housed, in dark, airless, unsanitary conditions where diseases could, and did, spread like wildfire. Steerage passengers usually got no more than an hour a day on deck in daylight.

MASS GRAVES: The bodies of 6,000 dead Irish migrants were found in a common grave near Montreal in the 1850s when a new bridge was being built. A granite boulder marks the spot today – it is known locally as The Black Rock.

THE FENIANS AND THE 1867 RISING

In 1858 – 10 years after their rebellion – a number of former members of the Young Ireland movement founded the secret revolutionary nationalist movements, the IRISH REPUBLICAN BROTHERHOOD (IRB) in Dublin, and the FENIAN BROTHERHOOD in the USA. Members of both groups were known as 'Fenians'.

Their aim was to end British rule in Ireland with an army of Irish rebels. As the new movement grew in numbers, its leadership began to plan for an armed rebellion. Among its members were two men who would have a major influence on Irish history: Michael Davitt, founder of the LAND LEAGUE, and John Devoy, who, from the USA, helped organise the 1916 Rising.

THE FENIAN RISING

The Fenians were different from other Irish revolutionary organisations because of the involvement of a number of men who had immigrated to the USA and fought in the American Civil War, which took place in the 1860s. Some of these men came back to Ireland to join the rebellion. But even so, it was a miserable failure, betrayed by informers and bad leadership.

THE MANCHESTER MARTYRS

In an IRB attempt to release two Irish American Fenian leaders from a prison van in Manchester, a British police sergeant, Charles Brett, was accidentally killed. Three captured Fenians, William Allen, Michael Larkin and William O'Brien, were convicted of Brett's murder and publicly hanged in Manchester in November 1867. As they left the court, they shouted 'God save Ireland' and have since been known to Irish nationalists as 'The Manchester Martyrs'.

WERE THE FENIANS THE FOUNDERS OF MODERN CANADA?

In addition to organising a very unsuccessful rebellion in Ireland, the Fenians took part in a number of raids on Canada in the 1860s. The idea was to hold it to ransom for Irish independence. (Stop laughing – I'm serious!) In 1866, a force of 1,300 Irishmen, accompanied by some Native Americans from the Mohawk tribe and African American Civil War veterans (I promise I'm not making this up) crossed into Canada and defeated Canadian troops in two battles before retreating to the USA. One effect of the raid was that it hastened plans for the formation of a Canadian government. So the Fenians have some claim to be Canada's Founding Fathers, right? OK, I admit that's a bit of a stretch ...

PIERCE NAGLE: BETRAYER OF THE FENIANS

The Dublin policemen who kept an eye on the IRB were well-informed about its activities thanks to their spy, Pierce Nagle. Nagle worked on the Fenian newspaper *The Irish People*. He testified at the trials of members of the IRB leadership in 1865. After giving his (disputed) evidence, he fled to England. London police believed that an unidentified body discovered in the East End of the city on 24 June 1866 was his, and that he had been murdered. If that was the case, the IRB kept very quiet about his killing ...

THE LAND WAR

Irish landlords have got a pretty bad rap over the years. Many deserved it, but most probably did not. Aside from the famine period, when the number of evictions soared, the removal of tenants from their land was quite rare and generally didn't happen until they were far behind in their rent.

The exception was when economic conditions were bad. This happened all over again in the period of the so-called **LONG DEPRESSION** (1873–1896), which began in the USA and caused food prices to fall in Europe. This made it difficult for Irish farmers to pay their rent, and in the late 1870s the rate of evictions began to climb back towards levels not experienced since the famine. The response in some areas was the violent resistance of secret societies of tenant farmers (called **RIBBONMEN**), who often murdered landlords and their agents, as well as those farmers who took over land from which families had been evicted. (The farmers who took over land were called **LAND GRABBERS**.)

THE LAND LEAGUE

Mayo was the county worst affected by the agricultural depression (and by years of awful weather one after the other), and it was there that ex-IRB member Michael Davitt formed the Land League, a non-violent political organisation. When it expanded throughout the country, he offered the leadership of the league to the young up-and-coming nationalist MP Charles Stewart Parnell. At a series of public meetings, and in the House of Commons, Parnell argued for rent reductions. He won the argument when British Prime Minister William Gladstone set up a **LAND COURT** in 1881. The court travelled around the country fixing fair levels of rent. After rents were lowered by an average of 15 to 20 per cent, the violence in the countryside faded for a few years – until food prices dropped again in the mid-1880s and the whole cycle kicked off again. This continued until the British government began to get rid of the landlords by lending money to the tenant farmers to buy their land. The farmers would eventually own the land themselves when they paid back their loans.

THE LAND FOR THE PEOPLE !

THE THREE FS

What Irish tenant farmers had been struggling for since the mid-19th century was the 'Three Fs': **FAIR RENT** (a rent they could afford to pay even in bad times), **FIXITY OF TENURE** (no evictions as long as they paid their rent), and **FREE SALE** (compensation, if they were evicted, for improvements they had made to their farm, like buildings and sheds). The British prime minister, William Gladstone, introduced two new laws, the Land Acts of 1870 and 1881, which largely granted the Three Fs, much to the annoyance of many landlords.

CAPTAIN BOYCOTT

One of the main weapons the Land League used against landlords, agents and land grabbers involved doing absolutely nothing! No one would speak to them, work for them or sell food to them. One of the earliest victims of this practice was the Mayo land agent Captain Charles Boycott. A Mayo priest, aware that many of his mostly Irish-speaking parishioners could not pronounce the word 'ostracisation' (which described what the locals were doing to their enemies) hit on the idea of calling it 'boycotting' instead. The English language had a new word, though Captain Boycott himself wasn't exactly thrilled at this form of immortality.

SPOTLIGHT ON
ANNA PARNELL

In October 1881, Charles Stewart Parnell and the leadership of the Land League found themselves in Kilmainham Jail with no prospect of getting out until the Ribbonmen stopped committing acts of violence in rural Ireland. Just for good measure, the government also banned the Land League. It was replaced by the Ladies' Land League, led by Parnell's younger sister, Anna.

Born in 1852, Anna Parnell was an extraordinary person. A woman's place back then was in the home, not on a public platform or risking arrest for political acts.

She led the Ladies' Land League in providing support for evicted families. She once ran into the middle of a Dublin street, stopped the horse of the lord lieutenant, Earl Spencer, and scolded him for the policies of the government of which he was a member.

Many Land League leaders, including Michael Davitt, thought she was fiercer and far more effective than her more famous brother, Charles. When he was released from prison in May 1882, he rewarded Anna by shutting down the Ladies' Land League, accusing it of having spent too much money. He ignored the fact that much of the money had been spent on providing tasty meals for the Land League prisoners in Kilmainham Jail. After that rebuke from her own brother, Anna Parnell bowed out of politics and never spoke to him again. It was Ireland's loss.

MOTHER JONES

Mary Harris Jones was born in Cork in 1837 and went on to become renowned, not in her native Ireland, but in the USA. Her family moved to Canada when she was five, and she settled in Memphis, Tennessee, in 1861. Much of her early life was marked by tragedy. In the 1860s, she lost her husband and four children to the horrible disease of yellow fever. She was qualified as a teacher but worked as a dressmaker instead and became involved in fighting on behalf of working men and women in the 1870s. She toured

the country campaigning for laws that would ban the employment of children in coal mines.

She led strikes and encouraged workers to 'pray for the dead, and fight like hell for the living'. Employers who paid very low wages to their workers didn't like her. To them she was 'the most dangerous woman in America'. She was an 'agitator', someone who prodded people into taking action to improve their lives. To the people she fought for, she became 'Mother Jones'. As she

grew older, her hair got whiter and she became more motherly looking, but she wasn't any less fierce in her fight against millionaires who exploited men, women and children.

Someone once tried to insult her by calling her 'the grandmother of all agitators'. Jones took it as a compliment and responded, 'I hope to live long enough to become the great-grandmother of all agitators.' She managed to achieve that by living until the age of 93.

HOME RULE

Charles Stewart Parnell had always had one main aim – to make Ireland independent from Britain. He wanted this to happen legally, rather than through violence. This meant the British government would have to be persuaded to pass a law making Ireland free and independent – called the HOME RULE ACT. The king or queen of England, however, would still be the head of state.

But when he became leader of the nationalist IRISH PARLIAMENTARY PARTY (IPP) in 1880 his goal seemed very far away. He started with the smaller goal of helping Irish farmers to get the Three Fs, particularly fair rents. He managed to achieve this in 1882. His next step was to establish a large and organised political party with so many MPs that they would have to be listened to in the House of Commons in London.

THE 86 OF '86

In 1886 his hard work paid off and his party won 86 seats. Because the two parties running for government were neck and neck, his party held the 'BALANCE OF POWER' and could choose which British party would become the government. William Gladstone, the leader of the Liberal Party, said he would give Ireland its own government, so Parnell supported him and Gladstone became prime minister again. Although Gladstone did try to have a law passed giving Ireland its own government, not enough MPs supported him and it was defeated.

THE FALL OF PARNELL

Soon after he became the leader of the Irish Parliamentary Party, Parnell started going out with a woman called Katharine O'Shea. She was actually married to one of his colleagues – Captain William O'Shea – but they did not get on well and had decided to live apart. Captain O'Shea was an unpleasant character – he was fond of himself and didn't mind breaking rules if it helped him to get ahead. He knew his wife was living with Parnell (they lived together for ten years, so he couldn't have missed it!) but he was waiting for Katharine's rich aunt to die and expected to be rewarded when his wife inherited her fortune. When the old lady, 'Aunt Ben', eventually passed away at the age of 97, she made sure O'Shea couldn't get his hands on a penny. That was when he sued for divorce. This caused huge trouble for Parnell and cost him the leadership of his party in 1890. At that time, causing a divorce – Captain O'Shea blamed Parnell – was considered to be a big scandal. Parnell died the following year at the age of 45.

RICHARD PIGOTT THE FORGER

· · · · · · · · · · · · · ·

In 1887, *The Times* newspaper in London claimed that Parnell had supported a policy of murder during the Land War. They even printed a letter with his signature on it to try and prove it. But when it was investigated, they found that the letter had been forged and sold to the newspaper by a dodgy Dublin journalist, Richard Pigott. The forger fled and Parnell sued *The Times* for telling lies about him. He won £5,000, which was a lot of money in those days.

THE CULTURAL REVIVAL

After the O'Shea divorce case, the Irish Parliamentary Party split into supporters and opponents of Parnell. This divide did not heal even after Parnell died in 1891. As a result of this lack of unity, Irish people became fed up with politics. During the 1890s and early 1900s, cultural matters, like art, music, literature and sport, were more important to them. A number of organisations that were very influential during the later period of the IRISH REVOLUTION (1916–1921) came into being during this time.

Cumann Lúch Chleas Gael bunaithe 1884

THE GAELIC ATHLETIC ASSOCIATION

The traditional Irish sports of hurling/camogie and football (as well as handball and rounders) had been played for centuries. To come up with a common set of rules and to stop the spread of sports of British origin (the 'foreign games' of soccer, rugby, hockey and cricket) a number of men gathered in the Hayes Hotel in Thurles, County Tipperary, in 1884 to form an association that would support Gaelic games. They included Maurice Davin, who became the first president of the GAELIC ATHLETIC ASSOCIATION (GAA), and Michael Cusack, who became its secretary. In case you hadn't noticed, the GAA is still with us and it's doing rather well. Two of the stands in Croke Park are called after Cusack and Davin.

Lizzie J Hayes

CONRADH NA GAEILGE

By the 1890s, the Irish language was in crisis. The famine had had the worst effect on the poorer Irish-speaking areas of the country. English was the language of business, politics and the law. In 1851, almost a quarter of Irish people spoke the language regularly – 5 per cent of the population actually spoke no English at all! Forty years later, the number of Irish speakers was down to 15 per cent, and only one person in a hundred spoke no English. In 1893 the GAELIC LEAGUE/ CONRADH NA GAEILGE was established to stop this decline. By 1906 it had 900 branches and 100,000 members. The 1911 census showed that numbers of Irish speakers had not fallen any further since 1891. Among other things that we should be grateful to the Gaelic League for is having St Patrick's Day as a national holiday.

THE ABBEY THEATRE

The world-famous Abbey Theatre in Dublin was also founded at around this time by one of Ireland's Nobel Prize-winning poets, W.B. Yeats, and his friend Lady Augusta Gregory. The Abbey was founded to perform the work of young Irish playwrights and to stir up debates and controversy with these new plays. Its most famous writers were John Millington Synge and Sean O'Casey. Both Synge's *The Playboy of the Western World* (1907) and O'Casey's *The Plough and the Stars* (1926) annoyed some people so much that they caused riots among the first-night audiences. So Yeats and Lady Gregory must have been doing something right!

THE THREAT OF CRICKET

What do you think was the most popular sport in Ireland in the middle of the 19th century? Hurling? Sorry, wrong! Gaelic football? Nope! Rugby? Afraid not. Three strikes and you're out – and, no, it wasn't rounders either. The correct answer is cricket! It arrived in Ireland in 1792 with a match in the Phoenix Park between the 'Military of Ireland' and the 'Gentlemen of Ireland'. But it quickly shook off its military and upper-class origins and spread throughout the country. By 1855 an Irish cricket team was able to beat England by 107 runs! The rise of the GAA and the 1902 move to ban its members from playing 'foreign games' meant that the sport went into decline. But today's Irish cricket team is still able to beat England, so the sport hasn't gone away!

THE PLAYBOY of the WESTERN WORLD

J. M. Synge

THE PLOUGH AND THE STARS

A TRAGEDY IN FOUR ACTS

BY SEAN O'CASEY

IRISH WOMEN AND THE VOTE

After 1898, Irish women were allowed to vote in local elections. They still had no vote (known as SUFFRAGE) in general elections to the British House of Commons. In England, the Women's Social and Political Union, led by Emmeline Pankhurst, fought for women to get the vote in general elections. Our version was the IRISH WOMEN'S FRANCHISE LEAGUE (IWFL). This was led by Margaret 'Gretta' Cousins and Hanna Sheehy-Skeffington. At the time they were known as 'SUFFRAGETTES'.

THE IRISH WOMEN'S FRANCHISE LEAGUE

In June 1912, Hanna Sheehy-Skeffington and Gretta Cousins, with six other members of the IWFL, smashed windows in the General Post Office (GPO) and other government buildings to get publicity for their cause. They were arrested and jailed. The following month, the British prime minister, Herbert Asquith, came on a visit to Dublin. When two supporters of Emmeline Pankhurst attacked Asquith with an axe, they ended up in Mountjoy jail, where they went on hunger strike. They were joined in the strike by members of the IWFL. Irish and British women succeeded in getting the vote in the general election of 1918, but only for women over the age of 30. All men over 21 could vote.

GERALDINE MANNING

In 1913 a woman named Geraldine Manning walked into the Royal Hibernian Academy art gallery in Lower Abbey Street in Dublin and left a note beside a sculpture of John Redmond, the Irish nationalist party leader in the British parliament. The bust was on display as part of a major exhibition. The note read, 'Why didn't you get us votes for women, Mr Redmond?' Redmond was against women getting the vote. Manning also poured a pot of green paint over the bust. When she was arrested, she told the police, 'I thought it no harm to paint here.' She was fined for the offence but preferred to go to jail rather than pay the fine.

Why didn't you get us votes for women, Mr Redmond? A traitor's face is no adornment to our picture gallery!

GEORGIE FROST

'Georgie' was actually Georgina. She helped her father in his work as a clerk in a courthouse in Clare. When he retired in 1915, she was offered his job. However, the government stopped the appointment because they thought the job was unsuitable for a woman. She sued to keep her job, lost two court verdicts and was about to plead her case to the House of Lords in London when, in 1919, the government caved in and changed the law so that women could be appointed to jobs in the civil service. Her victory changed the law forever for Irish and British women. Ironically, even though she had taken on and beaten the British government, she lost her job again in 1923 after Irish independence, when the new Irish Free State took over the court system.

CLERK

A TENEMENT

In the late 19th century, many working-class Dubliners lived in fine old red-brick buildings. Unfortunately, they didn't live one family to a house, but one family to a room! The tenement buildings of Dublin were often houses abandoned by the aristocracy and sold to greedy landlords. They were reckoned to be the most miserable, squalid homes in Europe.

The census of 1911 showed that 26,000 families lived in Dublin tenements; 77 per cent of those lived together in a single room. Numbers like that made it easy for killer diseases to spread quickly in the unhygienic conditions. In 1913, run-down tenements on Church Street collapsed, killing seven people living there. In 1963, two people were killed when a tenement collapsed in Fenian Street, so Dublin slums are more recent than you might think.

CHURCH STREET, 1913: At 8.45 p.m. on Tuesday, 2 September 1913, a noise 'like a cannon's roar' ripped through Church Street in Dublin as Numbers 66 and 67 collapsed, leaving 7 people dead and more than 100 homeless. Had people not been attending a show in the Father Mathew Hall nearby, far more would have died.

HENRIETTA STREET: This is the most famous tenement street in Dublin. In the early 20th century, in 15 tenement buildings, the street housed more than 800 people! That's more than 50 people per house. Number 7 Henrietta Street had 104 inhabitants in 1911.

SLUM LANDLORDS: The Dublin Housing Inquiry, which followed the 1913 Church Street buildings collapse, revealed that 14 members of Dublin Corporation, which ran the city of Dublin, owned tenement buildings and 1 member owned 19 of them! Guess who didn't want to get rid of sub-standard housing.

STRUMPET CITY: James Plunkett's novel about the 1913 Lockout – a major strike led by labour leader James Larkin – traces the lives of a dozen characters in Dublin's tenements.

TB: The abbreviation for the dreaded disease tuberculosis, also called consumption. This killer disease spread like wildfire in cramped tenement conditions and killed thousands of Irish men and women before we began to beat it in the 1950s.

LIVING ROOM: This was exactly what it says. In our houses today, it would be the largest room. In tenements, for many families, it was the *only* room.

BASIN AND BUCKET: There was no running water in a tenement building so all washing was done in a single metal basin. The water was carried in from outside in a bucket.

TOILETS: There were no fancy flush toilets in a tenement. Toilets were outside in a back yard or in dark, stuffy basements.

SEAN O'CASEY: The famous Dublin playwright, who lived in the tenements himself, wrote some of his greatest plays (*Juno and the Paycock*, *The Plough and the Stars*) about Dublin working-class people.

THE HOME RULE CRISIS

The two factions of the Irish Parliamentary Party (IPP) finally kissed and made up in 1900 after a split of almost a decade. John Redmond, who had always supported Parnell, was put in charge of the united party while one of Parnell's firmest opponents, John Dillon, became Redmond's deputy. These two men would lead the IPP for the next 18 years.

In 1905, a Dublin journalist, Arthur Griffith, who thought the IPP was far too gentle in its demands for a separate Irish parliament, set up a rival political organisation that he called Sinn Féin ('Ourselves Alone'). Sinn Féin sought complete independence from the UK rather than just a Home Rule parliament in Dublin. Because this separate Irish parliament would still have the king or queen as Irish head of state, it would have to give in to the British government on a number of issues, claimed Griffith. No one really paid much attention to Sinn Féin for more than a decade. That would change after the party won a massive majority of the Irish seats in the 1918 general election.

'ROME RULE'

In the general election of 1910, Redmond's party won enough seats to have the 'balance of power'. They had enough MPs to decide who would form the next government. Once again they opted to support the Liberals, led by Herbert Asquith. He became prime minister and immediately began working on a new Home Rule Bill. However, this did not go down well with (mostly Protestant) unionists in Ulster, who considered themselves British and wanted nothing to do with a Home Rule parliament in Dublin. They believed that an independent Ireland would be dominated by the Roman Catholic church; that Home Rule would be 'Rome rule'.

WE WON'T HAVE HOME RULE

"For God and Ulster!"

THE ULSTER RESPONSE

The response of the Ulster unionists, led by Dublin-born barrister Edward Carson and his main ally James Craig, was to establish a military force (the **ULSTER VOLUNTEER FORCE**), which pledged to keep Ulster British. In 1912, it persuaded almost half a million unionists to sign a document known as the **SOLEMN LEAGUE AND COVENANT** — all those who signed up pledged to use 'all means necessary' to defeat Home Rule for Ireland.

[ALMOST] HOME RULE

When the Home Rule Bill became law (and was signed by the king) in 1914, Ulster was left as part of the United Kingdom due to the unionists' objections. This happened just as World War I began. It was agreed to suspend Irish Home Rule until the war ended. By the time that occurred, things had changed completely ...

THE 1913 LOCKOUT

While Home Rule was being hotly debated by unionists and nationalists, a trade union (an organisation that fights for the rights of workers) was involved in a row with many Dublin employers who paid their workers very low wages. The Irish Transport and General Workers Union (ITGWU), led by James 'Big Jim' Larkin, told its members to stop driving the city's trams (a type of LUAS back in 1913) during Dublin Horse Show week in August. In response, the employers locked the union members out of their jobs. They would only be allowed to come back to work if they left the union. The Dublin Lockout was a long and bitter struggle. It led to huge hardship in working-class parts of Dublin and resulted in a victory for the employers when the ITGWU members, watching their children go hungry, had no choice but to give in.

UVF

IRELAND AND THE GREAT WAR

World War I began in August 1914, with the German invasion of Belgium. Great Britain was afraid Germany would become too powerful if the invasion was successful. A massive drive began to get hundreds of thousands of volunteer soldiers to join the British Army in the Great War, as it was known at the time.

Recruitment began in Ireland in September 1914, and three new Irish military units called 'divisions' (with around 10,000 soldiers in each) were created. These were the 10th, 16th and 36th divisions. The 10th was a mixed (Catholic/Protestant–unionist/nationalist) division, the 16th was largely southern nationalist (Home Rule supporters) and the 36th was Ulster unionist. By 1915, all three divisions had been fully trained and sent into action. The first Irish division to suffer major casualties was the 10th, sent to GALLIPOLI to fight one of Germany's allies, the army of Turkey. The worst experience for the 10th was at a place called Suvla Bay in Turkey, where they lost hundreds of men.

THE BATTLE OF THE SOMME

On the first day of the Battle of the Somme in northern France (1 July 1916), the 36th (Ulster) Division found itself in the front line. It was spectacularly successful in crossing NO MAN'S LAND (the area between the two sets of enemy trenches) and taking the enemy positions opposite them. Tragically, this success was temporary. Most other British Army units made no progress. This allowed the Germans to concentrate on taking back the trenches they had lost to the Ulstermen. And that resulted in 2,000 dead soldiers from Northern Ireland.

In taking two small villages, Ginchy and Guillemont, in September 1916, the nationalist 16th (Irish) Division lost almost as many men as the 36th had on 1 July.

The gruesome Battle of the Somme lasted for five months, and the British and French managed to move forward the position of their trenches by only a few kilometres. It finally ground to a halt at the end of November 1916, leaving almost half a million men dead. That's nearly the population of County Cork.

THE BATTLE OF MESSINES

By 1917, the nationalist 16th and unionist 36th divisions were under the command of one of the best British generals, Herbert Plumer. He had a big moustache, looked a bit like a teddy bear, and was a leader who genuinely cared about his troops. At the battle of Messines – it's called Mesen today – in Flanders (the Dutch-speaking part of Belgium), the two Irish divisions had quite an easy victory with light casualties. The battle started with the explosion of 19 huge **UNDERGROUND MINES** under the German lines. One of the mines planted back in 1917 still hasn't exploded – no one knows where it is! One of the Irish dead, however, was the popular Major William Redmond, brother of the IPP leader John Redmond.

16TH (IRISH) DIVISION

36TH (ULSTER) DIVISION

10TH (IRISH) DIVISION

'TO MY DAUGHTER BETTY ... '

One of the best poems written during the Great War was by Dublin poet Thomas Kettle, who was killed at the Battle of Ginchy in September 1916. A few days before he died he wrote a beautiful sonnet (a poem of 14 lines) to his young daughter. He had become bitter after the bloody British reaction to the 1916 Rising and wanted his little girl to know why he had joined the British Army to, as he saw it, fight for Christian civilisation against barbarism. This is how the poem ends:

So here, while the mad guns curse overhead,

And tired men sigh with mud for couch and floor,

Know that we fools, now with the foolish dead,

Died not for flag, nor King, nor Emperor,

But for a dream, born in a herdsmen shed,

And for the secret Scripture of the poor.

THOMAS M. KETTLE
1880~1916
BORN IN COUNTY DUBLIN
9TH FEBRUARY 1880.
KILLED AT GINCHY
9TH SEPTEMBER 1916.
POET. ESSAYIST. PATRIOT.

WORLD WAR I TRENCHES

Within months, both sides on the Western Front of WW I (Britain and France vs. Germany) became bogged down. Neither side was strong enough to make any big gains of territory. The result was a stalemate – no one could make any progress – so they, quite literally, 'dug in'. The two sides built an almost continuous series of trenches from the Belgian coast to the French–Swiss border, more than 400 kilometres long!

The German trenches tended to be better built. They often had concrete underground rooms in which troops could shelter safely. But all the trenches on both sides were cold, wet, uncomfortable, rat-infested and disease-ridden and would not pass modern health-and-safety inspections. This was especially the case when the other side began lobbing over explosive shells or attacking across no man's land.

SANDBAGS: These were used in their thousands to shore up trenches and keep out water.

LICE: They just loved the unhygienic conditions in the trenches, with thousands of soldiers living close together and unable to bathe. They would leave blotchy red bite marks all over the men's bodies. They were often burned out of the troops' clothing with lighted candles or cigarettes, though the 'Tommy' (British soldier) had to be careful not to set his uniform on fire.

THE RITZ

DUG-OUT: This was a chamber dug into the trench walls. Often the German versions used concrete to make them less vulnerable to a direct hit from a shell. Only the senior officers could hang out in these.

NO MAN'S LAND: This was the area between the opposing trench lines. In some areas of the Western Front, they were only a couple of hundred metres apart. Elsewhere, the front lines could be separated by more than a kilometre.

SHRAPNEL SHELL: This would explode overhead and send hundreds of lethal missiles in all directions. It was very effective against troops attacking across no man's land.

TRENCH FEVER: One of the gifts – along with a horrible itch – of the lice, trench fever brought shooting pains and a high temperature. But it was not fatal, unlike the Spanish Flu of 1918, which spread like wildfire in the trenches, or typhus, which lice could also carry.

TRENCH FOOT: This condition was the painful result of soldiers' feet being immersed in water for too long. If you really want to know what it's like you can try it yourself, but we wouldn't recommend it. Get someone you don't like to do the experiment instead.

DUCK BOARDS: These were wooden boards placed along the bottom of a trench to make walking easier. Also, if kept dry, they helped soldiers avoid 'trench foot'.

TRENCH PERISCOPE: This device contained two small mirrors that allowed soldiers to see across no man's land without having to put their heads above the parapet (the top of the trench), something that was not a good idea.

THE 1916 RISING

One of the long-standing mottoes of the Irish Republican Brotherhood (aka the Fenians) was 'ENGLAND'S DIFFICULTY, IRELAND'S OPPORTUNITY'. This was based on the idea that the best time for a rebellion in Ireland was when British soldiers were otherwise occupied in one of the UK's many foreign wars.

PLANNING A REBELLION

World War I was, of course, the father and mother of all military distractions, and a group within the IRB, called the MILITARY COUNCIL, led by Patrick Pearse, Thomas Clarke and Seán MacDermott, thought there was no better time to organise a rising against British rule than right in the middle of the Great War. So plans were made for a rebellion during Easter week, 1916. The soldiers were to come from the IRISH VOLUNTEERS, a nationalist military organisation formed shortly after Carson and Craig had set up the unionist Ulster Volunteer Force.

Contact was made with the old Fenian John Devoy in the USA. At this point, America was not involved in the Great War, and Devoy was able to negotiate with Germany to provide arms for the Rising. The IRB also discovered that the tiny IRISH CITIZENS' ARMY (which was founded to protect Dublin workers during the 1913 Lockout) was planning a rising of its own. Its leader, James Connolly, was kidnapped and agreed to co-operate with the IRB–Volunteers rebellion.

EASTER WEEK

The Irish Volunteers gathered regularly for (military) training events, but in reality they were secretly practising for a rebellion. On Easter Sunday, their leader, Eoin MacNeill, ordered all these 'training events' to be cancelled when he heard that a German naval ship, **THE AUD**, carrying weapons for the rebels, had been captured. But Pearse, Clarke, MacDermott and Connolly wanted to go ahead with their plans. So on Easter Monday, 1916, 2,000 Irish Volunteers ignored MacNeill and took a number of key buildings around the centre of Dublin. Their headquarters was in the General Post Office, outside of which Pearse read a **PROCLAMATION** declaring an Irish republic. The British government sent thousands of troops to Dublin. One of those units, the Sherwood Foresters, suffered around 200 casualties at Mount Street Bridge near Merrion Square as they made their way from Dún Laoghaire port to the city centre. But the rebels, who had taken the British by surprise at first, were badly outnumbered and outgunned and just couldn't hold out. By Saturday, 29 April, Pearse realised that the game was up and ordered all Volunteer units around the city to lay down their arms and surrender. By then, much of the city centre of Dublin had been badly damaged and more than 600 people, mostly civilians, had been killed.

THE 1916 EXECUTIONS

Ireland was placed under military rule and the army decided to make an example of the rebel leaders. Pearse and Clarke were two of the first to be executed. Most people assumed the shootings by firing squad would end after the 7 men who had signed the Proclamation of the Republic had been executed. But the British Army didn't stop at that number, and a total of 14 men, some not very prominent in the IRB or the Volunteers, were shot at dawn over a period of more than a week. At first the Rising had not been popular in Dublin, but the executions led to a reaction against Britain. There was particular disgust at the shooting of James Connolly. He had been badly wounded in the fighting and had to be strapped to a chair before being shot by a firing squad. The only important leader to survive was Eamon de Valera, who was spared when British Prime Minister Asquith ordered that the executions should be stopped.

NURSE ELIZABETH O'FARRELL

By Saturday, 29 April, the 1916 rebels had been forced to abandon their headquarters in the GPO. The time had come to avoid further bloodshed and give up the fight. But how to negotiate a surrender? Up stepped one of the most courageous women of the Easter Rising, 32-year-old nurse Elizabeth O'Farrell. She had already spent much of the week, along with her life partner Julia Grenan, risking her life delivering messages from the GPO to the other Irish Volunteer positions around the city.

Armed only with a Red Cross flag and a white flag of truce, she left the temporary Moore Street HQ and walked towards a British machine-gun position. Only when the white flag was recognised did the firing stop. When she reached the British lines, she was taken to meet the OC (officer commanding) of the British forces in Dublin, Brigadier-General William Lowe. He sent her back to Patrick Pearse with a demand for a total Volunteer surrender.

Then Pearse accompanied O'Farrell to meet Lowe at the top of Moore Street. A photographer recorded the scene, but just as he took his shot Elizabeth O'Farrell stepped back and only her feet can be seen in this famous photograph. The rest of her body was blocked by Pearse. Later, when the photograph was reproduced, her feet were often airbrushed out of the shot.

Elizabeth O'Farrell was then driven around Dublin, dropped at British military barricades and made to walk under a white flag to Volunteer positions to deliver the surrender document to all the other Volunteer units. Here was an opportunity for anyone with a rifle to, quite literally, 'shoot the messenger'. In addition to the danger from snipers, the angry Volunteer leaders, who didn't want to surrender, were not very welcoming. But Elizabeth O'Farrell behaved with great dignity as well as courage in persuading Volunteer commanders, like Eamon de Valera, that the time had come to give up the fight.

SPOTLIGHT ON
WINIFRED CARNEY

Winifred Carney was born in County Down in 1887 but moved to Belfast when she was a child. Like Mother Jones in America, Winifred became a trade unionist in the cloth-making textile industry. In Belfast, she met James Connolly and became his friend, adviser and secretary. On Easter Monday, 1916, she marched into the GPO at Connolly's side, armed with a typewriter and a revolver. She was the only woman present on day one but was joined later by Elizabeth O'Farrell and Julia Grenan. She never left Connolly's side until the surrender. Winifred was captured by the British after the Rising ended and was jailed in England. She was released just before Christmas 1916 and remained active in politics. She took the anti-treaty side in the Irish Civil War, during which she spent much time in jail. She died in Belfast in 1943 at the age of 55.

THE RISE OF SINN FÉIN

In September 1914 the future of Sinn Féin did not look very bright. John Redmond and the IPP had achieved a measure of Home Rule for Ireland. As a 'thank you' to the British government, Redmond encouraged Irish nationalists to join the army and fight in the Great War.

By the end of April 1916, thousands of his supporters had died. Then came the Irish disgust at the executions of so many of the leaders of the 1916 Rising. Although Sinn Féin had played no part in the Easter Rising, it was still called the 'Sinn Féin rebellion' by British soldiers and politicians who didn't know any better. That did the party no harm at all! Finally, in 1918, a desperate British government, at risk of losing the Great War, tried to apply CONSCRIPTION (compulsory army service) to Ireland. Suddenly things were not looking so bright for the Irish Parliamentary Party, led by John Dillon since Redmond's death in March 1918. Although the IPP had opposed conscription as well, it was Sinn Féin that got most of the credit for the successful campaign to defeat it.

THE REBELS RETURN

Many 1916 rebels were sent to a prison camp in north Wales called FRONGOCH. When they were released in 1917 they were welcomed back with open arms in huge demonstrations. Eamon de Valera replaced Arthur Griffith as president of Sinn Féin, and the party went on to win a number of seats in the British parliament in BY-ELECTIONS (elections that take place when an MP dies in office or resigns).

THE 1918 ELECTION

The Great War ended on 11 November 1918. One of the first things the British government did was to call a general election. There hadn't been one since 1910. This time, all men over the age of 21 were entitled to vote, as were women over the age of 30. Twenty-six unionist candidates (including Edward Carson) won seats, mostly in Northern Ireland. Otherwise it was a straight contest between the revolutionary republicans of Sinn Féin and the much more moderate Home Rulers of the IPP. The revolutionaries did spectacularly well. Sinn Féin took 73 of the 105 Irish seats. The IPP was reduced to just 6 seats!

THE FIRST DÁIL

Sinn Féin had no intention of taking the seats it had won at Westminster. Instead, its MPs met in the Mansion House in Dublin on 21 January 1919 as the very first DÁIL ÉIREANN. Here the Sinn Féin MPs became TDs (TEACHTA DÁLA) and pledged their support and allegiance to an Irish republic. In April 1919, Eamon de Valera became president of the IRISH REPUBLIC at the second meeting of Dáil Éireann.

THE (NOT SO) GREAT ESCAPE

In May 1918, de Valera (Dev) was arrested. He was put into prison in England, in Lincoln jail. While serving Mass there, he managed to make a wax impression of the prison chaplain's key to an outside gate. He then sent a home-made cartoon Christmas card to Dublin. This featured a life-size drawing of the key (I kid you not!). A few weeks later, a key, copied from the card, was sent in a cake to Lincoln prison. (Oh, come on, everyone knows that old trick!) But it was the wrong size. It took a number of cake deliveries to get the right key. (Many more of them and Dev would have been too big to squeeze through the gate.) Then, on the night of the escape, de Valera's outside helpers managed to break their key in the gate's lock. Dev managed to force it out and use his own key to make his escape.

THE WAR OF INDEPENDENCE

On the day Dáil Éireann met in Dublin in January 1919, a group of Tipperary IRISH VOLUNTEER members (later the Volunteers were known as the IRISH REPUBLICAN ARMY – the IRA) killed two policemen at Soloheadbeg. Two of the Volunteers, Dan Breen and Sean Treacy, would become almost legendary figures in the conflict that followed.

The Soloheadbeg killings pushed both the British and the Volunteers into the two-and-a-half-year-long Irish War of Independence. This was mostly fought on the Irish side by IRA 'Flying Columns' of 30 to 50 men who would strike at the police or the British Army (the crown forces) and then retreat into hiding.

MICHAEL COLLINS

While the 1916 survivor Cathal Brugha was the Sinn Féin Minister for Defence, and the top commander of the IRA, it's another member of the Sinn Féin leadership, Michael Collins, who is better remembered. Collins was Director of Intelligence, which meant he was tasked with finding out everything about the crown forces. He ran a superb spying operation in Dublin and defied all the efforts of the police to catch him, even though he often cycled around the city right under their noses.

BLOODY SUNDAY, 1920

One of the most deadly operations organised by Collins was a series of co-ordinated attacks on a number of British agents in Dublin at 9 a.m. on Sunday, 21 November 1920. This led to 15 killings – though not all the dead were British spies – and shocked the British government to its core. Later that day, members of an elite unit of the British crown forces, known in Ireland as the BLACK AND TANS (because they wore black police tunics and khaki or tan trousers), retaliated by attacking the crowd at a football match between Dublin and Tipperary in Croke Park. Thirteen spectators and one of the members of the Tipperary team, Michael Hogan (after whom the Hogan Stand is named), were killed.

THE TRUCE

The War of Independence was a bitter conflict, with many civilian deaths and brutal revenge killings by both sides. There was also widespread damage to property, as members of the crown forces burned the centre of Cork city as well as the towns of Balbriggan, County Dublin, and Trim, County Meath. The British government carried out a number of executions, the most notorious being the hanging of 18-year-old IRA member Kevin Barry in Dublin in November 1920. After two and a half years, it was clear that neither side was going to win, so a truce was agreed and both parties began the talks in London that would lead to Irish independence.

THE SQUAD

Known also as the 'Twelve Apostles' (because of their number, not their holiness), the Squad was a small group of paid assassins recruited by Michael Collins. They were used to kill spies, informers, members of the crown forces and the police deemed by Collins to be a danger to the IRA and the Dáil. Their most notorious 'hit' was on a man named Alan Bell, who was investigating how the IRA got its money and where it was being banked. He was taken off a tram in broad daylight by members of the Squad and shot dead on the street in the Ballsbridge suburb of Dublin. The Squad members were also heavily involved in the killings on the morning of Bloody Sunday.

THE IRISH CIVIL WAR

In October 1921, a group of Irish rebels led by Michael Collins and Arthur Griffith travelled to London to negotiate the ANGLO-IRISH TREATY with Britain. The treaty they settled on in December would give 26 of the 32 Irish counties their independence but keep 6 northern counties for Britain.

As well as that, all TDs would still have to swear an OATH OF ALLEGIANCE to the king. It was a big compromise. There was not going to be a republic. Collins and Griffith put the terms of the treaty to the Dáil and it was passed by the very narrow margin, for such a vital decision, of 64 votes to 57. The IRISH FREE STATE came into being after the treaty vote was passed, but many TDs, including Eamon de Valera and Cathal Brugha, were unhappy and would not accept the result. They remained loyal to the idea of an Irish republic, so were called REPUBLICANS.

THE FOUR COURTS OCCUPATION

Two-thirds of the membership of the IRA also opposed the Anglo-Irish Treaty. An armed group of republicans seized the Four Courts building in Dublin in April 1922. When the Free State government, under Collins, used British artillery to blast them out of the building at the end of June 1922, the Civil War began. Within days, the Free State army managed to push the republican forces out of the capital city. Cathal Brugha was killed in the Dublin fighting.

THE END OF THE WAR

Over the next few months the republicans also lost Ireland's other major cities. Limerick fell to the Free State army on 20 July. Cork was taken on 10 August. After that, the republican forces, led by Liam Lynch, were forced to fight the same kind of war the IRA Flying Columns had fought against the British: hitting the Free State army in surprise attacks and ambushes. Then, in April 1923, Liam Lynch was killed in a skirmish in Tipperary. A few weeks later, his successor, Frank Aiken, ordered his men to lay down their arms. The bitter Irish Civil War was over. More than 2,500 had died in the conflict.

THE CIVIL WAR IN KERRY

Some of the worst fighting of this horrible war took place in County Kerry, where members of the Free State army were responsible for a number of awful murders of captured republican prisoners. The Free State government also executed more than 80 captured republicans held in the country's prisons, and there were a number of brutal attacks on women suspected of helping the republican forces. It took many decades for the bitterness left by the conflict to disappear.

WHO SHOT MICHAEL COLLINS?

One of those who died in the Civil War was Michael Collins. After years of escaping capture and execution at the hands of the British, Collins's luck finally ran out when he was shot dead in a skirmish at Bealnablath in his native Cork on 22 August 1922. Since his death there have been many rumours and theories about who fired the fatal shot. Some people even claim that he was shot accidentally by a drunken member of his own side! The bullet that killed him came from a distance of over 150 metres as daylight faded. So whoever fired it was either a deadly sniper or just very lucky indeed. Over the years, most people's money was on an ex-World War I sniper, Denis 'Sonny' O'Neill. But it now turns out that he had come back from the Great War with a severely disabled right arm. Though, presumably he could still pull a trigger or he wouldn't have been carrying a rifle. But it leaves the question wide open once again. Who shot Michael Collins? Sorry, I hope you weren't expecting an answer, were you?

A RURAL IRISH COTTAGE

In the early 1900s Ireland was still a very rural country, with most people making a living from farming. Although nearly 10 per cent of Irish houses in 1911 had 10 or more rooms, these were the exception. Far more typical was the rural Irish thatched cottage with one or two rooms, a kitchen and a whitewash finish on the outside walls. Many had no foundations and had mud or clay floors. The fireplace was usually at the centre of the cottage. Set into an outside wall, it served both as hearth and stove. The fire was never allowed to go out. Is it any wonder that the Irish version of 'There's no place like home' is 'Níl aon tinteán mar do thinteán féin' ('There's no hearth like your own hearth').

ASS AND CART: This was the most common way to transport goods and people. Only the wealthy could afford a horse and trap or (bliss) a carriage.

TURF STACK: You didn't buy this from Bord na Móna – you cut and saved it yourself from a local bog. If there was no bog nearby, the turf stack might be a wood pile.

DRESSER: This was generally found in the better-off homes in rural Ireland. It was a large wooden storage unit with shelves for dishes and drawers for kitchen utensils (and for hiding your dinner if someone called at the wrong time).

CHICKENS: No image of a rural Irish home would be complete without at least a couple of chickens clucking around, providing the occasional egg or, when they had outlived their usefulness, ending up in one of those big iron pots!

THATCHED ROOF: Many Irish cottages had roofs thatched with dry vegetation like straw or reeds. The thatch was layered to keep out water and provide good insulation. It would regularly be replaced by a visiting thatcher, who had probably learned his skills from his father or grandfather.

KITCHEN GARDEN: Whether you were a livestock or crop farmer, or owned one of the many local pubs (generally in your front room), most cottages had a small area out the back used for growing everything from mint to potatoes.

CAST-IRON POTS AND PANS: These were heavy and long-lasting, and were suspended over the open fire for cooking.

BEAN AN TÍ: This means 'woman of the house' – the absolute ruler of the traditional Irish cottage (despite what her husband might think) and your hostess should you ever visit the Gaeltacht.

OPEN HEARTH FIRE: This was located in the kitchen and used for cooking as well as for heating the house.

PUMP: Few houses had one of their own – most were public pumps in the middle of a village. Like Jack and Jill, you often had to travel up a hill to fetch your pail of water.

THE KETTLE: This was never far from the open fire and always available for brewing the exotic concoction imported from India during the days of the empire ... tea.

IRELAND AFTER INDEPENDENCE

The 1920s was a pretty bleak time for the newly independent Irish Free State. The country's new leader, W.T. Cosgrave, led a very Catholic and very conservative government (CUMANN NA NGAEDHEAL). There had been a lot of physical damage to the country from 1916 to 1923, there were very few jobs, and the government had very little money – so much so that one of their first moves in 1924 was to reduce the old-age pension from ten shillings a week (about €150 today) to nine shillings to save money. ANTI-TREATY REPUBLICANS (who held on to the name Sinn Féin) refused to take their seats in the Dáil because they would have to take an oath of allegiance to the king.

FIANNA FÁIL

Then, in 1926, de Valera and a number of his supporters split from Sinn Féin. They formed a party named Fianna Fáil and took their seats in the Dáil. In 1932 they won the general election, but things didn't really get much better. With few jobs available in a largely agricultural economy, thousands of young Irish people emigrated each year.

THE BLUESHIRTS

A leading supporter of Cumann na nGaedheal, Eoin O'Duffy, who was in charge of AN GARDA SÍOCHÁNA in 1932, didn't want to see Fianna Fáil taking power but was overruled by Cosgrave. He was fired as Garda Commissioner soon after Fianna Fáil took office and formed an organisation of former Civil War Free State soldiers known as the NATIONAL GUARD. They marched and paraded regularly, to the annoyance of the government. Because of the colour of their uniforms they became known as the 'Blueshirts'. The Blueshirts quickly fizzled out as a threat to the Fianna Fáil government and disbanded in 1935.

IRELAND AND WORLD WAR II

As part of the Anglo-Irish Treaty the UK had held on to three Irish ports and stationed British navy vessels in each. In 1938 de Valera managed to persuade the UK to hand the ports back. His timing was excellent. Within months the **WORLD WAR II** had begun and Ireland, with no British gunboats in its waters for the German army to attack, was able to remain neutral. Although thousands of Irish men and women joined the UK armed forces and fought against **NAZI GERMANY**, the country itself chose not to take sides and possibly avoided a German invasion as a result.

THE MOTHER AND CHILD SCHEME

The Catholic Church had tremendous political power in post-independence Ireland and had almost total control of health and education. An example of this power was how the archbishop of Dublin, John Charles McQuaid, was able to get the government to abandon the Mother and Child Scheme in 1951. The plan, introduced by Health Minister Dr Noël Browne, would have given free medical care to mothers and young children. This was seen by McQuaid as a threat to Catholic Church control of the country's medical system. He was so powerful that his opposition led to the scheme being scrapped by the government and to the resignation of Noël Browne.

'THE LAUGHTER OF HAPPY MAIDENS'

Irish life in the 1930s and 40s was very different to our lives today. There was no TV or internet for a start. In fact, there were very few phones (and you couldn't carry them with you either). Most people still lived in rural Ireland. Cattle and sheep were sold in the larger towns at weekly 'fairs', where local farmers would take over the main street for the day. If you wanted to get around, your best bet was a bicycle – only the well-off had cars. Much of the entertainment was provided by *céilí* bands playing traditional jigs and reels, though there were some jazz bands (frowned upon by the Catholic bishops) in the cities. Eamon de Valera, who was Taoiseach from 1932–1948, once made a famous speech in which he praised this simple Irish lifestyle and the idea of 'the contest of athletic youths and the laughter of happy maidens' that he associated with this now distant and forgotten period of Irish life.

THE TROUBLES

The Irish Free State became the REPUBLIC OF IRELAND in 1949. The Free State had claimed to own Northern Ireland, and this continued when it became a republic. When it was established in 1920, Northern Ireland had twice as many unionists as nationalists.

Catholic nationalists in Northern Ireland felt abandoned and many never fully 'bought in' to the new state. In the late 1950s, the Irish Republican Army began to attack targets in the six counties in an attempt to achieve a united Ireland. This so-called 'BORDER CAMPAIGN' was abandoned in failure in 1962.

THE CIVIL RIGHTS MOVEMENT

Catholics were often at a disadvantage when it came to things like public housing and many felt like their CIVIL RIGHTS – the rights to social freedom and equality – were not being met. In the late 1960s, inspired by Dr Martin Luther King and the US African American Civil Rights Movement, a campaign began for Catholic civil rights in Northern Ireland. A number of large demonstrations took place, some of which were attacked by extreme unionists and by the largely Protestant police force, the ROYAL ULSTER CONSTABULARY (RUC). In 1969, as tensions increased, rioting erupted across Northern Ireland, with intense violence and killings in the city of Belfast. The British government sent in the army to restore law and order. They remained there for the next 30 years.

THE IRA CAMPAIGN

The IRA had not been active since the end of the border campaign in 1962. But in 1969, when Catholic areas in Belfast were attacked, it quickly came back to life. With the political support of the Sinn Féin party, the IRA began to attack British troops and members of the Northern Irish police force, the RUC. In response to this threat, there was also a revival of violent unionist organisations like the **ULSTER VOLUNTEER FORCE** (UVF) and the **ULSTER DEFENCE ASSOCIATION** (UDA). With the aim of bringing about a united Ireland, the IRA began to target and kill members of the RUC, unionist and British politicians, and members of the British armed forces with bullets and car bombs. The UVF and the UDA responded by killing IRA members whenever the opportunity arose, as well as targeting Catholic civilians. On a couple of occasions they used car bombs to kill people in the Republic of Ireland. Over the course of the **THE TROUBLES**, as this period of violence came to be known, around 3,500 people died. More than half were civilians, a third were members of the security forces, and the rest were loyalist and republican members of **PARAMILITARY** organisations – illegal groups that were organised like armies.

THE HUNGER STRIKES
·········

Jailed IRA members considered themselves to be political prisoners, or prisoners of war. The British government treated them as common criminals. IRA members who were forced to wear prison uniforms began a series of protests in the early 1980s in the Maze Prison in County Down, where most of them were held. This campaign eventually led to a number of hunger strikes, the most famous of which was that of Bobby Sands. He died on 5 May 1981 after refusing food for 66 days. Nine further Maze prisoners died before some of their demands – including the right to wear their own clothes – were met by the British government led by Margaret Thatcher. Both sides claimed victory.

THE GOOD FRIDAY AGREEMENT

The IRA bombs of the 1970s and '80s killed many hundreds of people. Some, like the killing of the Queen's relative Lord Mountbatten in 1979, were aimed at well-known targets. Others, like the bombing of the La Mon restaurant in Belfast in 1978, where 12 diners died, seemed to have no rhyme or reason whatever. But still the campaign continued, with the loyalist side also carrying out terrible attacks, such as the Dublin and Monaghan bombings of 17 May 1974, where four bombs killed 33 innocent people in the Republic of Ireland.

OUR GLORIOUS DEAD

1914-1918

1939-1945

ENNISKILLEN

Perhaps the IRA operation that angered and upset people more than any other was the Enniskillen, County Fermanagh, bombing on 8 November 1987 at a ceremony to remember WW I. The target was a British military band. Instead, ten local people and a policeman were killed. The dignified response of one of the injured victims, Gordon Wilson, whose daughter Marie died as he held her hand, struck home. In an emotional radio interview he forgave her killers.

JOHN HUME

While the IRA campaign continued in the 1980s, John Hume, the leader of the SDLP, a party that favoured a united Ireland by peaceful means, took a huge risk in holding secret talks with the Sinn Féin president, Gerry Adams. Hume encouraged Adams to persuade the IRA to stop their campaign of bombing and killing. When the general public became aware of the meetings in 1993, Hume was severely criticised for even talking to the Sinn Féin leader. But in 1994 the IRA ended their campaign of violence by declaring a CEASEFIRE. This resulted in talks that included Sinn Féin and led to the Belfast or Good Friday Agreement in 1998.

THE GOOD FRIDAY AGREEMENT

In 1998, talks began among the main northern political parties, as well as the Irish and British governments, to end the conflict in Northern Ireland. The main unionist party at the time, the Ulster Unionist Party, led by David Trimble, agreed to participate despite the involvement of Sinn Féin. The talks were very tough and almost broke down many times, but eventually all sides signed up to a historic agreement on 10 April 1998. This happened to be Good Friday, hence the name by which the deal is known today. There were still some hurdles to jump before the IRA gave up its weapons, but that followed two years later. Under the terms of the agreement, the Republic of Ireland had to give up its claim to Northern Ireland. David Trimble and John Hume were jointly awarded the 1998 NOBEL PEACE PRIZE.

OMAGH

Not all members of the IRA were prepared to go along with Sinn Féin's acceptance of the Good Friday Agreement. A splinter group calling itself the 'Real' IRA wanted to continue the bombing campaign. On 15 August 1998 (a busy Saturday) some of its members parked a stolen car with 230 kilos of explosives in the centre of Omagh, County Tyrone. The bomb went off at 3.10 p.m., killing 29 people and injuring 220. It was the deadliest single incident of the Troubles, killing Protestants and Catholics, southerners and northerners, children and adults, a woman who was pregnant with twins, and two Spanish tourists. If anything, it drove the parties that had signed the Belfast Agreement closer together.

THE CELTIC TIGER

The 1980s was a very bleak decade for the Irish economy. Unable to get jobs, thousands of young people emigrated. Things began to pick up in the 1990s, however. This was helped by the fact that Ireland, an English-speaking member of the EUROPEAN UNION – which we'd joined in 1973 when it was the EUROPEAN ECONOMIC COMMUNITY – offered a low tax rate for manufacturing companies. Some giant US companies opened European headquarters in Ireland. By the end of the decade the Irish economy was booming. Wages were rising and it was easier to get a job. This period became known as the CELTIC TIGER.

PROPERTY, PROPERTY, PROPERTY

One of the results of this 'BOOM' (where people seemed to be very well off) was that house prices began to increase at a dizzying rate. People living in modest homes discovered that their properties were worth hundreds of thousands of euros. Many Irish people were then able to borrow money because their houses were worth so much, and they used that money to buy other properties. Some bought houses or apartments in Ireland that they then rented out. Others bought foreign properties and holiday homes in Europe and even further afield. Banks were almost throwing money at anyone who wanted to borrow it. House values continued to climb for almost a decade – preventing a lot of younger and poorer people from buying homes – and it seemed as if they would just keep on climbing. Until they didn't ...

THE CRASH

This 'boom' Irish economy of the nineties and the 'noughties' was based almost entirely on the fact that people *felt* wealthy. They only had to look at the value of their house, after all. One bank, **ANGLO-IRISH**, which had been tiny in the 1980s, had grown colossally based on loans made to property developers, who build, buy and sell properties. The other Irish banks had also given out billions of euros in similar loans. What goes up, must come down, and from 2008 that's exactly what happened. It all began with the collapse of American banks, and the panic quickly spread to Europe. Irish property prices began to fall, and then to tumble. Every major Irish bank found itself in trouble. The government couldn't allow the banks to fail or the economy would seize up, but neither could it afford to cover their losses, particularly those of Anglo-Irish Bank, now floating on a stormy sea of debts without sails or a paddle. Ireland had to be rescued by a global banking organisation known as the **INTERNATIONAL MONETARY FUND** (IMF), at a cost to the Irish government of €64 billion. This had to be paid back by the Irish people, many of whom had bought second and third properties now worth only a fraction of what they had paid for them. It took barely a decade for thousands of Irish people to become property millionaires (on paper!). It took almost another decade for the country to recover from the madness of the Celtic Tiger.

THE EUROVISION SONG CONTEST

. . . .

During the Celtic Tiger, it seemed that nothing could go wrong for the Irish. Irish actors were winning Oscars; Irish sportspeople were winning medals and championships. But the strangest success story of all was how we just kept winning the Eurovision Song Contest. Between 1987 and 1996 we won five of the ten contests, including three in a row between 1992 and 1994! In 1994, the Irish-dance show *Riverdance* was performed as the interval act, and it soon became a worldwide sensation. Since then, we've been accused of entering a number of turkeys because we haven't triumphed in over 25 years. And, of course, we definitely did enter one in 2008 when Dustin the Turkey, star of RTÉ TV's *The Den*, competed on our behalf with the song 'Irlande Douze Pointes' (Ireland Twelve Points – that's the maximum number of votes you can get from any of the competing countries). Sadly, Dustin's incredible talent just wasn't recognised by the European juries and he crashed out in the semi-final, finishing joint 15th of 19 countries.

SILICON DOCKS

The Dublin Docklands stretch eastwards along the Liffey from the Matt Talbot Bridge, taking in the classic Custom House, the 3Arena and the port of Dublin. It's an area that has altered radically in the last 30 years. In 1990, although it was losing trade to other big Irish ports like Belfast and Warrenpoint, it was beginning to develop in other directions. The establishment of the International Financial Services Centre (IFSC) in the 1980s and the opening of the Point Theatre in 1988 were among the first signs of change. Then the tech boom of the early 2000s, and Ireland's low tax rate for corporations, created 'Silicon Docks' by bringing many of the giant tech companies of Silicon Valley in California to the area, as well as the LUAS and the *uber*-cool Samuel Beckett Bridge. The Dublin Docklands Development Authority is responsible for the area.

THE EPIC IRISH EMIGRATION MUSEUM: If the *Jeanie Johnston* doesn't float your boat (Yes – that was deliberate!) you can discover many more Irish emigrant stories in the EPIC museum on the Custom House Quay.

THE CONVENTION CENTRE: Opened in 2010, it has brought dozens of major events to the city of Dublin. The rest of us got to see inside when Dáil Éireann moved there during Covid-19 so that politicians could be even more distant from each other than they are in Leinster House.

THE JEANIE JOHNSTON: As a reminder of the way we were, this replica of a famine ship is permanently docked in the Docklands, where it operates as a museum of famine and emigration. The original *Jeanie Johnston* carried 2,500 impoverished Irish emigrants to America in very different times indeed.

THE CUSTOM HOUSE: More 1790s than 1990s, this beautiful building designed by the famous 18th-century architect James Gandon has been a landmark fixture at the entrance to the Docklands area since it was completed in 1791.

RIVER LIFFEY

CARGO SHIPS: These were the most frequent visitors to the area around Dublin port in the 1990s.

THE POINT THEATRE: The smaller cousin of the 3Arena opened in 1988 on the site of a former railway goods handling station. Then it got too small ...

THE CENTRAL BANK: Originally intended as the headquarters of Anglo-Irish Bank, those plans changed when Anglo-Irish went spectacularly bust in 2011 and almost brought the country with it. Instead, the shell of the building was redesigned for the Central Bank.

3ARENA: This is the upgraded and enlarged Point Theatre, capable of holding 13,000 concert fans. In 2012 it was the fourth busiest arena in the world. Among the acts to have sold out the venue are Billie Eilish, Ariana Grande and Demi Lovato.

FACEBOOK: The California social-media giant followed Google to the so-called Silicon Docks

GRAND CANAL DOCKS

TWITTER: Couldn't leave them out, now, could we? They are there too. About the only major social-media company not in the Silicon Docks these days is the networking giant LinkedIn. No, wait a minute, they're there too.

BORD GÁIS ENERGY THEATRE: Originally the Grand Canal Theatre, it lies on the south side of the Liffey and was designed by the famous American architect Daniel Libeskind.

GOOGLE: The European headquarters of the internet giant, established in 2002, now employs 3,500 people.

A MILLION YEARS OF IRISH HISTORY

ROUND ONE

Circle the correct answer

1. What did the Megalosaurus eat as it cavorted near the Giant's Causeway in County Antrim?
a) Green salad b) Bagel and cream cheese c) Grass d) Meat

2. The woolly mammoth was once found in Ireland?
a) True b) False

3. In what Irish river valley would you find Newgrange, Knowth and Dowth?
a) The Boyne b) The Nile c) The Thames d) The Shannon

4. When did St Patrick begin his mission to Ireland?
a) Sunday b) 432 BC c) AD 33 d) AD 432

5. How did the Viking chieftain Ivar the Boneless get his name?
a) He had no bones b) Nobody knows c) He was spineless d) He chose it himself

6. In which Irish county would you find Tara?
a) Meath b) Worcestershire c) Torremolinos d) Cork

7. What was the name of Strongbow's wife, the daughter of Dermot MacMurrough?
a) Murrough b) Aoife c) Aisling d) Mrs Strongbow

8. Which movie was filmed around Trim Castle in 1994?
a) *Frozen* b) *Harry Potter and the Slim Castle* c) *Mad Max* d) *Braveheart*

9. With what instruments was the sport of 'horlings' played?
a) A net and oval ball b) Two snooker cues c) Stick and ball d) A deck of cards

10. Silken Thomas was known for his love of what?
a) Fine clothing b) Parallel parking c) Harry Potter books d) Fine wines

11. What was Cromwell's suggested alternative destination, after 'hell', for defeated Irish landowners?
a) Ibiza b) Connacht c) A hole in the ground d) Dublin

12. What was the name of the wife of King William III and daughter of King James II?
a) Mary b) Elizabeth c) Rhiannon d) Taylor

13. Where would you find this stone?

a) The Eiffel Tower b) 10 Downing Street c) Tara d) Newgrange

14. What do you call this water-filled area around a Norman castle?

a) A moat b) A groat c) A stoat d) A float

15. Who is this? (Clue: he's the least popular Englishman in Ireland by a country mile)

a) Boris Johnson b) Oliver Cromwell c) Nigel Farage d) King Charles I

ANSWERS:
1.d) 2.a) 3.a) 4.d) 5.b) 6.a) 7.b) 8.d) 9.c) 10.a) 11.b) 12.a) 13.d) 14.a) 15.b)

ROUND TWO

Circle the correct answer

1. What is the name of the famous Palladian mansion in Celbridge, County Kildare?
a) The Albert Hall b) The 3Arena
c) Castletown House d) Russborough House

2. By what initials was the informer Leonard McNally known to Dublin Castle?
a) M b) USA c) BMW d) JW

3. With which Irish leader did John d'Esterre fight a duel in 1815?
a) Daniel O'Connell b) Daniel O'Donnell c) Brian O'Driscoll
d) Charles Stewart Parnell

4. What was the name given to the huge meetings held during the repeal campaign in 1843?
a) Massive b) Minimal c) Monster
d) Modest

5. What was the population of Ireland before the Famine?
a) 800 million b) 8.2 million
c) 2.1 million d) 80

6. Which British prime minister was responsible for the first Home Rule Bill?
a) Benjamin Disraeli b) William Gladstone c) Eamon de Valera
d) Boris Johnson

7. In which town was the GAA founded in 1884?
a) Thurles b) Dublin c) New York
d) Cairo

8. Who became Director of Intelligence in the first Sinn Féin government in 1919?
a) Cathal Brugha b) Mary Lou McDonald c) Michael Collins
d) Arthur Griffith

9. What was the name of the political party formed by Eamon de Valera in 1926?
a) Sinn Féin b) The Republican Party
c) Fianna Fáil d) The Social Democrats

10. Of which Northern Ireland party was John Hume the leader for many years?
a) SDLP b) Greens c) DUP d) Sinn Féin

11. On which day was the 1998 Belfast Agreement signed?
a) Bloody Sunday b) Good Friday
c) Christmas Day d) Spy Wednesday

12. The collapse of which bank meant the end of the Celtic Tiger?
a) The Central Bank b) The West Bank
c) The Left Bank d) Anglo-Irish Bank

13. Who is this? (Clue: He became leader of the Irish Parliamentary Party and fell out with his sister Anna)

a) Roy Keane b) Daniel O'Connell
c) Charles Stewart Parnell
d) Edward Carson

14. Dustin the Turkey won the Eurovision Song Contest for Ireland in 2008.
a) True b) False

15. What is the name of this ship?

a) The *Asgard* b) The *Titanic*
c) The *Britannia* d) The *Jeanie Johnston*

ANSWERS: 1. c) 2. d) 3. a) 4. c) 5. b) 6. b) 7. a) 8. c) 9. b) 10. a) 11. b) 12. d) 13. c) 14. b) 15. d)

91

INDEX

Gill Books
Hume Avenue
Park West
Dublin 12
www.gillbooks.ie

Gill Books is an imprint of M.H. Gill and Co.

978 0717 94926

Designed by Graham Thew
Edited by Emma Dunne
Proofread by Michelle Griffin
Printed and bound by Firmengruppe APPL, Germany
This book is typeset in Hatch.

The paper used in this book comes from the wood pulp of sustainably managed forests.

A CIP catalogue record for this book is available from the British Library.

5 4 3 2 1

FSC
www.fsc.org

MIX
Paper | Supporting
responsible forestry
FSC® C004592

COLLECT THEM ALL

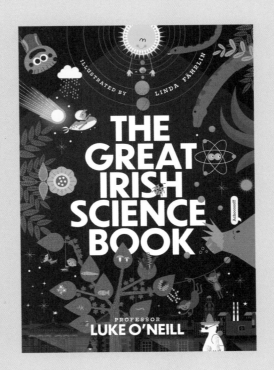

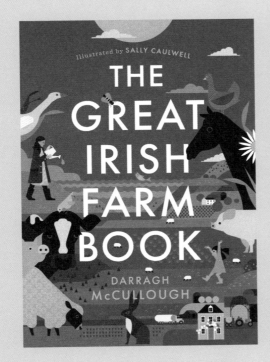

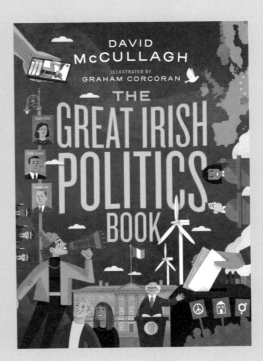